OCR
Research Methods for Psychology
AS & A2

Moira Donald with Louise Ellerby-Jones

HODDER
EDUCATION
AN HACHETTE UK COMPANY

Orders: please contact Bookpoint Ltd, 130 Milton Park, Abingdon, Oxon OX14 4SB.
Telephone: (44) 01235 827720. Fax: (44) 01235 400454. Lines are open from 9.00-5.00,
Monday to Saturday, with a 24-hour message answering service. You can also order through our
website www.hoddereducation.co.uk

If you have any comments to make about this, or any of our other titles, please send them to
educationenquiries@hodder.co.uk

British Library Cataloguing in Publication Data
A catalogue record for this title is available from the British Library

ISBN: 978 1 444 12342 5

First Published 2011
Impression number 10 9 8 7 6 5 4 3 2 1
Year 2015, 2014, 2013, 2012, 2011

Hachette UK's policy is to use papers that are natural, renewable and
recyclable products and made from wood grown in sustainable forests.
The logging and manufacturing processes are expected to conform to the
environmental regulations of the country of origin.

Cover photo © Image Source/Getty Images

Typeset by Dorchester Typesetting Group Ltd
Printed in Great Britain for Hodder Education, An Hachette UK Company,
338 Euston Road, London NW1 3BH

Contents

Introduction   v

Part One: OCR AS Unit G541: Psychological Investigations   1

Chapter 1 Approaches and perspectives   2

1.1 Cognitive approach   2

1.2 Physiological approach   5

1.3 Social approach   8

1.4 Individual-differences approach   10

1.5 Developmental approach   11

1.6 Behaviourist perspective   13

1.7 Psychodynamic perspective   15

Chapter 2 Methods of data collection and analysis   17

2.1 The experimental method   17

2.2 The observational method   28

2.3 Self-report   36

2.4 Correlation   40

Answers   44

Chapter 3 Issues in psychological investigations   48

3.1 Ethics   48

3.2 Reliability and validity   51

3.3 Hypotheses   56

3.4 Variables   58

3.5 Sampling   60

3.6 Procedures   65

3.7 Data analysis   73

Answers   80

Part Two: OCR A2 Unit G544: Approaches and Research Methods in Psychology   95

Chapter 4 Designing a practical project   96

4.1 Selection and construction of a research question   96

Answers   110

Chapter 5 Approaches, perspectives and debates for A2   117

5.1 Format of section B (Approaches, perspectives and debates)   118

5.2 Forensic Psychology examples: approaches and perspectives   119

5.3 Health and Clinical Psychology examples: approaches and perspectives   121

5.4 Sport and Exercise Psychology examples: approaches and perspectives   123

5.5 Psychology of Education examples: approaches and perspectives   126

5.6 Debates in psychology   128

5.7 Using your knowledge in Unit G544   130

Chapter 6 Research methods for A2   141

6.1 Format of section B (Research Methods and Issues)   141

6.2 Examples of the experimental method (laboratory and field)   142

6.3 Examples of the observational method   144

6.4 Examples of the self-report method   144

6.5 Examples of the correlational method   145

6.6 Case-study method   146

6.7 Using your knowledge in Unit G544: Answering research methods and issues questions   148

Bibliography   159

Index   162

Introduction

This book has been written for students following the OCR AS and A2 Psychology courses. It is designed to support the *Psychology AS for OCR* and *Psychology A2 for OCR* textbooks, by helping to ensure you are fully prepared for your Psychological Investigations paper at AS and your Approaches and Research Methods paper at A2, and that you are on track to get those top marks.

The OCR exam structure is set out below:

The OCR AS Exams

Psychological Investigations
This is a 1-hour written paper accounting for 60 marks (30 per cent of the total AS marks). It is formed of three sections, A, B and C, and candidates will be required to answer all questions.

Core Studies
This is a 2-hour written paper accounting for 120 marks (70% of the total AS marks). It is formed of three sections: in section A candidates are required to answer all questions, and then one question from both section B and section C.

The OCR A2 Exams
The OCR A2 level assessment is formed of two exams:

Options in Applied Psychology
This will be a 2-hour written paper accounting for 100 marks (50 per cent of the total A2 marks). It is formed of four options: forensic psychology, health and clinical psychology, psychology of sport and exercise and psychology of education. You will be required to answer two questions from two of these options.

Approaches and Research Methods in Psychology
This will be a $1\frac{1}{2}$ hour written paper accounting for 80 marks (50 per cent of the total A2 marks). It is formed of two sections: in section A you will be required to answer all the questions; in section B you will answer one question from a choice of two.

There are three assessment objectives:

AO1, Knowledge and Understanding
- recognise, recall and show understanding of scientific knowledge;
- select, organise and communicate relevant information in a variety of forms, including extended prose.

AO2, Application of Knowledge and Understanding
- analyse and evaluate scientific knowledge when presenting arguments and ideas;
- apply scientific knowledge to unfamiliar situations including those related to issues;
- assess the validity, reliability and credibility of scientific information;
- bring together scientific knowledge from different areas of the subject and apply them.

AO3, Science in Practice
- demonstrate ethical, safe and skilful practical techniques selecting appropriate qualitative and quantitative methods;
- know how to make, record and communicate reliable and valid observations and measurements with appropriate precision and accuracy, through using primary and secondary sources;
- analyse, interpret, explain and evaluate the methodology, results and impact of their own and others' experimental and investigative activities in a variety of ways.

Walkthrough
There are a number of consistent features that appear throughout the book to help you make the most of your learning:

Extend Your Understanding
Key definitions and concepts that you should make sure you understand.

Core Study Example
Explicit links between the research methods material you are learning and the Core Studies.

Questions and Answers
Throughout the book there are sample questions and sample answers, and in chapters 2, 3 and 4 there are some questions for you to have a go at yourself. Possible answers can be found at the end of these chapters.

Please bear in mind when using the sample questions and answers, that the answers given are not designed to be perfect top-band answers. They are to point you in the right direction when you are thinking about the topics. You will have to use your own knowledge and the guidance given in this book to reach for those top marks.

About the authors
Moira Donald is Head of Psychology at the Stephen Perse Sixth Form College in Cambridge. Moira recently graduated in Experimental Psychology from the University of Oxford, following a previous career as a university lecturer.

Louise Ellerby-Jones is an examiner for a leading awarding body and a teacher of psychology at the Highfield School, Letchworth. She is an active member of the Association for the Teaching of Psychology.

Acknowledgements
The author would like to thank staff and students from the Stephen Perse Sixth Form College, especially Libby Ahluwalia and Paul Fannon; Judith Silver from Camden School for Girls; Jane Mellanby, Ann Dowker, Kate Nation and Jenny Yiend from the Department of Experimental Psychology, University of Oxford, and also the Psychology editorial team at Hodder Education.

Part One
OCR AS Unit G541: Psychological Investigations

Chapter 1 Approaches and
perspectives   2

Chapter 2 Methods of data collection
and analysis   17

Chapter 3 Issues in psychological
investigations   48

Introduction

This book is the research methods companion to *Psychology AS for OCR* and *Psychology A2 for OCR* by Louise Ellerby-Jones, Karon Oliver and Moira Donald. This book can be used in preparation for the OCR Psychology units G541: Psychological Investigations and G544: Approaches and Research Methods in Psychology, and should also prove useful for revision of the Core Studies for AS and the Applied Options for A2. The book is divided into two sections: the first focusing on preparing for Psychological Investigations and the second containing the additional material necessary for the synoptic paper, G544: Approaches and Research Methods. The book as a whole is necessary preparation for G544.

1 Approaches and perspectives

1.1 Cognitive approach   2
1.2 Physiological approach   5
1.3 Social approach   8
1.4 Individual-differences approach   10
1.5 Developmental approach   11
1.6 Behaviourist perspective   13
1.7 Psychodynamic perspective   15

The OCR specification for AS focuses on five psychological approaches – **Cognitive, Physiological, Social, Individual Differences** and **Developmental Psychology** – and two psychological perspectives – **Behavourism** and the **Psychodynamic** perspective. You may wonder what the difference is between an approach and a perspective. The words are in this context more or less synonymous (i.e. they mean the same thing), but OCR distinguishes between them for examination purposes. The five named approaches are the focus of G542: Core Studies and each one is represented by three studies in the syllabus. The perspectives are historically important approaches in psychology that are no longer central to most modern academic research but are still used by applied psychologists and also underlie some of the assumptions made in the other approaches. Although G541: Psychological Investigations does not contain questions on the approaches and perspectives, it is important to go over the basic elements of each of the five approaches and two perspectives in order to understand the research methods that relate to each one. For those who choose to go on to study Psychology at A2, this section provides a necessary background for answering section B of G544: Approaches and Research Methods in Psychology.

1.1 Cognitive approach

Cognitive psychology is one of the main contemporary approaches in psychology. It is the study of internal mental processes and their effects on behaviour.

Some key assumptions of the cognitive approach

Assumptions means key beliefs that are fundamental to an approach:

- That mental processes can be studied scientifically
- That mental processes shape behaviour
- That the brain stores, processes and retrieves information rather as a computer does (although the ways in which the processing systems work are not that similar).

What do cognitive psychologists study?

Cognitive psychologists study the whole range of mental processes. Sensory perception, attention, memory, language and emotion are some of the key focuses for research. The three cognitive approach studies that you meet at AS deal with memory (**Loftus and Palmer, 1974**), emotion perception (**Baron-Cohen** *et al.*, **1997**) and language (**Savage-Rumbaugh** *et al.*, **1986**).

What research methods are used in cognitive psychology?

In Chapter 2 the various research methods used by psychologists will be examined in more detail. In this chapter we will discuss the methods used in each approach. The four main research methods that you need to understand for G541 are as follows:

- Experiment
- Observation
- Self-report
- Correlation.

[handwritten: data collection]

[handwritten: hypoteza / przypuszczenie – data analysis]

See Chapter 2 for explanations of the above research methods.

One further research method that you will come across at AS is the case-study method. A case study is an investigation that is conducted with a small number of participants, often over a period of time, to enable in-depth collection of data. In case studies other methods are used to collect the data, including experiments (usually quasi-experiments, observations or self-report). You do not need to identify or define the case-study method for Psychological Investigations but we will return to case studies in Chapter 6.

It is important to note that the first three methods are methods of data collection while the fourth method, correlation, is a method of data analysis, not a method of data collection.

It is also important to note that these methods are not mutually exclusive. Researchers may conduct an experiment that depends in part on data collected by self-report. Data collected using the self-report method are often analysed using correlational techniques.

Extend Your Understanding

Data

Data are the facts and figures that researchers collect and analyse in order to test their ideas and theories. Data collection is undertaken through experiments, observational studies and self-report measures, e.g. questionnaires. Data can be either quantitative (numerical) or qualitative (descriptive).

More information on data analysis can be found in Chapter 3. 3.7, p.73.

All four of the above techniques may be used in the cognitive approach but the most frequently used method in cognitive psychology is the experiment. This is because the experimental method enables us to prove a causal relationship between two variables.

Core Study Example

Loftus and Palmer (1974) examined the effect of using different verbs to describe a car crash shown in a video on people's memory of the crash.

Extend Your Understanding

Variables *[handwritten: – zmienne]* *[handwritten: czynniki]*

The term variable simply means factor, but in psychology you need to use the specific term 'variable' when discussing factors involved in shaping behaviour. Proving a causal relationship between variables means being able to show that one variable (variable A) is directly exerting an influence on another variable (variable B) and the relationship is not reciprocal (i.e. variable B does not exert an influence on variable A). If two variables are shown to be related to each other but you cannot prove the direction of influence, we say that the variables are correlated (related). Cognitive psychologists often apply correlational analysis if they have used a method other than an experiment to collect their data.

For more information on variables, see Chapter 3. 3.4, p.58.

Another method used by cognitive psychologists is self-report. This will be discussed in more detail in Chapter 2. In summary it means that you use questionnaires or interviews to collect people's thoughts, feelings, ideas or memories.

Core Study Example

Baron-Cohen *et al.* (1997) asked people with autism, Tourette's syndrome and healthy controls to respond to questions about the emotions/mental states shown in the eyes of people photographed. This is self-report because the participants reported their thoughts about what other people must have been feeling.

Food for Thought

Cognitive psychologists do not usually use the observational method. Can you think why this might be the case?

Although cognitive psychologists tend not to use the observational method, there are exceptions.

Cognitive–approach psychologists sometimes apply correlational analysis when they cannot test for cause and effect. This is particularly true when a study uses physiological measures (e.g. brain scans). Increasingly, cognitive psychologists use data obtained via these methods, but we do not have a cognitive Core Study example of this approach.

Core Study Example

Savage-Rumbaugh *et al.* (1986) examines the development of language in bonobos (pygmy chimpanzees) using the observational method. Why do you think the researchers chose to use the observational method in their research?

Key strengths and weaknesses of the cognitive approach

Research undertaken in any approach can have strengths or weaknesses, depending on how well the researchers have adopted ethical guidelines and have fulfilled the basic requirements of fair and objective data collection and analysis. Nevertheless, it is possible to identify some of the key advantages and potential minefields that are general to each approach.

More information on ethics can be found in Chapter 3, 3.1, p.48.

Table 1.1 Strengths and weaknesses of the cognitive approach

Strengths of the cognitive approach	Weaknesses of the cognitive approach
The cognitive approach applies rigorous, scientific approaches to the study of mental processes and how they shape behaviour.	The cognitive approach frequently deals with inner processes that are not observable. This means that researchers are often dependent on **self-report** for their data and such data are not always seen as **objective**.
Example:	Example:
The cognitive approach enables us to gain insights into inner processes that are not observable behaviours.	Although the cognitive approach helps us theorise about the way in which mental processes occur it is not usually directed at answering questions about the physical processes that underlie processes, such as how memories are stored in the brain.

Table 1.1 continued

Strengths of the cognitive approach	Weaknesses of the cognitive approach
Example:	Example:
Cognitive-approach studies often use the experimental method, which enables identification of causes of specific behaviours.	Cognitive-approach studies often use the experimental method, which can limit the **ecological validity** of the findings.
Example:	Example:

NB: Gaps have been left for you to identify Core Studies that are examples of studies that show the strengths and weaknesses described above. When you have studied all three of the cognitive-approach Core Studies, try to fill in these gaps.

Extend Your Understanding

Objectivity/subjectivity

When people allow their emotions, biases or prejudices to influence their judgement or their data collection, this is termed **subjectivity**. When judgements are based on data that have been collected by controlled, scientific methods and the findings analysed without prejudice, they are seen as **objective**. The goal of a scientist is to be as **objective** as possible. However, dealing with human nature is not an exact science and some psychologists value **subjective** insights.

Extend Your Understanding

Ecological validity

When researchers conduct studies, one of their goals is to ensure that the way in which the research is conducted is as close to real-life situations/behaviour as possible. When this is achieved, the study is described as being **high** in **ecological validity**. When the procedure is removed from real life the study may be criticised for being **low** in **ecological validity**.

For more on the issue of ecological validity, see Chapter 3, p.54.

1.2 Physiological approach

The physiological (biological) approach is one of the main contemporary approaches in psychology. It is the study of the physical correlates of behaviour.

Extend Your Understanding

Physical correlates

Physical correlates are the physical processes in the brain regions that can be identified as **relating to** particular behaviours.

Some key assumptions of the physiological approach
- That what is psychological is first biological
- That behaviours have physical correlates
- That behaviour can be largely explained in terms of biology (genes/hormones).

What do physiological psychologists study?

Physiological psychologists study the physical processes that underlie mental processes and behaviour. Neurotransmission, hormones, brain localisation and genetics are some of the key focuses for research. (For an explanation of these topics, see *Psychology AS for OCR*, *Psychology A2 for OCR* and *OCR A2 Psychology Key Studies Companion*. The three physiological approach studies that you meet at AS deal with sleep and dreaming (**Dement and Kleitman, 1957**), hemispherical specialisation in the brain (**Sperry, 1968**) and localisation of brain function (**Maguire *et al.*, 2000**).

What research methods are used in physiological psychology?

Of the four main research methods (experiment, observation, self-report and correlation) the key ones used in physiological psychology are correlations and experiments, although observations and self-report techniques are sometimes also used in conjunction with physiological data collection.

Research methods in physiological psychology have changed enormously over the past 10–15 years. Two of the Core Studies (**Dement and Kleitman, 1957** and **Sperry, 1968**) are classic studies that were conducted many years ago without the benefit of modern technology. Dement and Kleitman and Sperry used a case-study approach that adopted as far as possible an experimental or quasi-experimental method. Maguire *et al.* is a more up-to-date study that uses the latest brain-scanning technology (Magnetic Resonance Imaging) in quasi-experimental and correlational analysis. The most frequently used method in physiological psychology today is correlation. This is mainly because of the popularity of brain-scanning studies. These studies indicate correlations between behaviours or mental processes and particular areas of the brain that show activations during scans.

> ### Core Study Example
> **Maguire *et al.* (2000)** examines differences in taxi drivers' brains as compared with non-taxi drivers. Part of this study examines the relationship between time spent as a taxi driver and the relative mean difference in hippocampal volume between the two groups. This is a correlation because the researchers were unable to test for cause and effect.

Another frequently used method in physiological psychology is the experiment or quasi-experiment.

Extend Your Understanding

Quasi-experimental method

True experiments are ones in which the experimenter manipulates the independent variable (IV) and measures the dependent variable (DV). This is discussed in more detail in Chapter 2. When the experimenter does not manipulate the IV but examines the effect of naturally occurring differences (e.g. gender, clinical condition, life experience) on a dependent variable, the study should be regarded as a quasi-experiment rather than a true experiment. Often physiological studies compare the results of tests or scans on an experimental group with pre-existing data from a representative cross-section of the normal population (control) rather than the experimenter going out and finding a control group of the same size as the experimental group.

For more information on IVs and DVs, see Chapter 3, 3.4, p.58.

Core Study Example

Maguire *et al*. (2000) scanned 16 taxi drivers and then compared their findings with scans of 50 normal individuals in the hospital database who were not taxi drivers.

Sometimes observational procedures are used to investigate behaviours in clinical groups.

Core Study Example

Sperry (1968) conducted a study on patients who had surgery for epilepsy. This was a case study in which the researcher observed the patients while they were put through tests of vision and other perceptual abilities.

Sometimes physiological data and self-report data are collected and compared.

Core Study Example

Dement and Kleitman (1957) collected physiological data (EEG recordings – see *Psychology AS for OCR* for further details) on sleeping participants together with self-report data of dream recall.

Table 1.2 Strengths and weaknesses of the physiological approach

Strengths of the physiological approach	Weaknesses of the physiological approach
The physiological approach enables us to understand the biological basis of human behaviour.	Physiological research is often correlational, which means that cause and effect cannot be identified.
Example:	Example:
Recent advances in both genetic research and the application of modern technology (e.g. MRI/fMRI scans) have greatly extended our understanding of how biology shapes behaviour.	Physiological psychologists are sometimes criticised for reductionism* because they reduce behaviours to specific physical processes.

Table 1.2 continued

Strengths of the physiological approach	Weaknesses of the physiological approach
Example:	Example:
The physiological approach is generally scientific and uses rigorous controls and objective data-collection techniques.	Physiological psychologists are sometimes criticised for determinism** because they attribute behaviours to innate physiological factors rather than to choice/free will.
Example:	Example:

*/**For AS level it is not necessary to understand reductionism or determinism so these concepts are discussed in more depth in the A2 section of this book.

NB: Gaps have been left for you to identify Core Studies that are examples of physiological studies that show the strengths and weaknesses described above. When you have studied all three of the physiological-approach Core Studies, try to fill in these gaps.

1.3 Social approach

Social psychology is one of the main classical approaches in psychology. It is the study of human interactions and group behaviour.

Some key assumptions of the social approach
- That humans are social animals and human behaviour can be best understood in terms of interpersonal relationships
- That explanations of human behaviour should take into account situational factors as well as individual factors because context and culture influence behaviour
- That individuals do not always exercise free will but are often influenced in their behaviours by others.

What do social psychologists study?

Social psychologists study human behaviour in a social context. They often focus on group dynamics, interpersonal relations and how people interpret and deal with the behaviour of others. The social approach studies that you meet at AS deal with obedience (**Milgram, 1963**), conformity to roles (**Reicher and Haslam, 2006**) and helping behaviour (**Piliavin, Rodin and Piliavin, 1969**).

What research methods are used in social psychology?

Of the four main research methods (experiment, observation, self-report and correlation) the key ones used in social psychology are observations and experiments, although self-report techniques are also used.

(1) Social psychologists often use observational techniques, although these are sometimes incorporated into an experiment.

Core Study Example

All three social-approach Core Studies use observational techniques. **Milgram (1963)** recorded people's reactions to the stressful situation in which he placed them for his quasi-experiment. **Reicher and Haslam (2006)** kept the participants in their prison simulation under constant observation and recorded their reactions to the roles they were allocated. **Piliavin, Rodin and Piliavin (1969)** in their field experiment placed observers in a subway carriage to record details such as the race and gender of those who helped the 'victim' and the period of time that elapsed before help was given.

(2) The experiment is a frequently used method in social psychology. However, social psychologists will sometimes use field experiments rather than laboratory experiments in order to study human behaviour in real-life settings.

Core Study Example

Piliavin, Rodin and Piliavin (1969) is an example of a field experiment in which participant variables were not controlled, although the experiments conducted a controlled procedure.

(3) Another method used by social psychologists is self-report.

Core Study Example

Reicher and Haslam (2006) administered self-report measures of mood in order to understand the impact of a prison simulation on participants' feelings.

Table 1.3 Strengths and weaknesses of the social approach

Strengths of the social approach	Weaknesses of the social approach
Social approach studies are often high in ecological validity because they study people in real-life situations.	Social psychologists have in the past sometimes broken ethical guidelines and risked causing psychological harm to participants. However, present-day social psychologists make every effort to maintain high ethical standards.
Example:	Example:
The social approach enables us to gain an understanding of the influence of situations and other people's actions on our behaviour.	Social psychologists do not always have control of variables as they study human interactions (using observations or field experiments) and these cannot be controlled in the same ways as, for example, cognitive tasks in laboratory experiments.
Example:	Example:

Table 1.3 continued

Strengths of the social approach	Weaknesses of the social approach
The social approach enables us to understand social cognition – in other words, what we think and feel about our own behaviour and the behaviour of others.	With the social approach it can be difficult to devise a reliable, valid measure of human interactions.
Example:	Example:

NB: Gaps have been left for you to identify Core Studies that are examples of social-approach studies that show the strengths and weaknesses described above. When you have studied all three of the social-approach Core Studies, try to fill in these gaps.

1.4 Individual-differences approach

The individual–differences approach is one of the most established approaches in psychology. It is the study of what makes individuals unique rather than what we as humans have in common.

Some key assumptions of the individual-differences approach

- That studying what makes us unique as individuals is as important as understanding norms of human behaviour
- That the differences between people in terms of personality and intelligence are important influences on behaviour as well as situational factors
- The individual–differences approach is fundamental to an understanding of mental health and dysfunctional psychology.

What do psychologists who take an individual-differences approach study?

Traditionally, the main focuses in individual-differences psychology are psychological disorders, personality and intelligence. The three individual-differences approach studies that you meet at AS all focus on dysfunctional psychology. **Rosenhan (1973)** is a study into the reliability of diagnosis of psychological disorders; **Thigpen and Cleckley (1954)** is a case study of reported multiple personality disorder; **Griffiths (1994)** explores the issue of gambling addiction.

What research methods are used in individual-differences psychology?

All of the four main research methods (experiment, observation, self-report and correlation) are used in individual–differences research but the key methods are probably the case study and self-report.

(1) Self-report is used frequently in the individual-differences approach.

> ### Core Study Example
> In **Griffiths (1994)** some participants were asked to verbalise their feelings and thoughts as they gambled. This is a self-report method that is met with less frequently than questionnaires and interviews. **Thigpen and Cleckley (1954)** conducted therapy with the participant and in their analysis they relied to a large extent on the patient's self-report of symptoms.

(2) Both laboratory and field experiments are used in the individual–differences approach.

> **Core Study Example**
>
> **Griffiths (1994)** is a laboratory experiment although conducted in the field (a gambling arcade). It is defined as a laboratory experiment because both participant and task variables were controlled.

(3) The observational method is sometimes used in the individual–differences approach.

> **Core Study Example**
>
> In **Rosenhan (1973)** experimenters playing the role of pseudopatients observed the behaviour of medical professionals towards themselves.

(4) Individual–differences psychologists sometimes apply correlation analysis to examine relationships between variables they cannot manipulate. For example it is possible to correlate personality and intelligence variables. However, none of the individual differences Core Studies in the AS course incorporates correlational analysis.

Table 1.4 Strengths and weaknesses of the individual-differences approach

Strengths of the individual-differences approach	Weaknesses of the individual-differences approach
The individual differences approach enables us to determine which aspects of human behaviour are general to the species and which are shaped by individual factors.	The individual-differences approach sometimes deals with very small sample sizes, which means the results are not generalisable.
Example:	Example:
The individual differences approach often uses a detailed case-study approach that provides rich data.	Individual-differences psychology may lead to labelling if individuals are categorised as different from the norm, with labels such as 'dysfunctional' , of 'low intelligence' or 'neurotic'.
Example:	Example:
The individual differences approach helps us understand issues of mental health and psychological dysfunction.	Psychometric tests attempt to measure traits such as intelligence and personality that may not really be amenable to measurement.
Example:	Example:

NB: Gaps have been left for you to identify Core Studies that are examples of individual-differences studies that show the strengths and weaknesses described above. When you have studied all three of the individual-differences approach Core Studies, try to fill in these gaps.

1.5 Developmental approach

Developmental psychology is one of the key established approaches in psychology. Developmental psychologists study cognitive and behavioural changes across the lifespan.

Some key assumptions of the developmental approach

- That cognitive abilities and processes are not static but that change occurs across the life-time
- That behaviour changes with age
- That methods developed in other approaches (e.g. cognitive, physiological) can be used to understand developmental change.

What do developmental psychologists study?

Traditionally focusing mainly on infancy and childhood, the remit of developmental psychology is now from birth to old age. Developmental psychologists can and do study just about anything that psychologists who use other approaches study, but always with regard to changes in cognition and behaviour over the lifespan. The three developmental approach studies that you meet at AS focus on children's reasoning (**Samuel and Bryant, 1984**), children's imitation of aggressive behaviour (**Bandura, Ross and Ross, 1961**) and Freudian analysis of childhood phobia (**Freud, 1909**).

What research methods are used in developmental psychology?

From what has been said above it is probably self-evident that developmental psychologists can use any of the key research methods.

(1) The most frequently used method today in developmental psychology is probably the cognitive experiment.

> ### Core Study Example
> **Samuel and Bryant (1984); Bandura, Ross and Ross (1961)** is a laboratory experiment that tests chidren's ability to conserve.

(2) Developmental psychologists also make frequent use of the observational method.

> ### Core Study Example
> **Bandura, Ross and Ross (1961)** used a structured observation within their experimental study. **Freud (1909)** used observations reported by Little Hans's father in producing his analysis of Hans's phobia.

(3) Another method often used by developmental psychologists is self-report, with the limitation that first-hand self-report is not possible in the case of very young children but instead an alternative self-report method is used by which adults familiar with a child respond to questions about the child's behaviour.

> ### Core Study Example
> In **Bandura, Ross and Ross (1961)**, the experimenter and the nursery teacher completed behavioural checklists of aggression in order to allocate the children to matched participant groups. **Freud (1909)** relied for his analysis on reports of Hans's behaviour made by his father.

(4) Developmental-approach psychologists sometimes apply correlation analysis when they wish to analyse the relationship between variables that they cannot manipulate. For example, correlations could be investigated between age of participants and number of correct responses on a cognitive test. However, none of the developmental Core Studies in the AS course incorporates correlational analysis.

Table 1.5 Strengths and weaknesses of the developmental approach

Strengths of the developmental approach	Weaknesses of the developmental approach
The developmental approach enables us to understand how cognition and behaviour change across the lifespan.	Much developmental research focuses on children and this raises ethical issues, particularly in the case of very young children who cannot give informed consent or understand debriefing.
Example:	Example:
The developmental approach often uses well-controlled studies such as experiments to investigate cognitive development.	Developmental psychology tends to focus on developmental norms and may underestimate the role of individual differences in development.
Example:	Example:
A case-study approach is sometimes used, which enables collection of rich longitudinal data.	There can be practical difficulties involved in working with children. It can be difficult to ensure that they understand instructions, they can have difficulty concentrating on tasks and they may be more subject to suggestion than adults.
Example:	Example:

NB: Gaps have been left for you to identify Core Studies that are examples of developmental studies that show the strengths and weaknesses described above. When you have studied all three of the developmental-approach Core Studies, try to fill in these gaps.

1.6 Behaviourist perspective

Behaviourism was the dominant psychological approach in the mid decades of the twentieth century. It still has some adherents (particularly in clinical psychology) but it is no longer one of the main approaches in academic research in psychology.

Some key assumptions of the behaviourist perspective
● That only observable behaviours can be subjected to scientific study
● That all learning is the outcome of stimulus–response relationships
● That all behaviours are learned, not innate.

What do behaviourist psychologists study?
Behaviourist psychologists study learning and behaviour. A study that incorporates behaviourist principles that you meet at AS is primarily **Bandura, Ross and Ross (1961)**, although some would argue that **Milgram** is behaviourist in the sense that obedience to authority may be seen as learned behaviour. For an alternative behaviourist perspective see the discussion of the case study of Little Albert (Watson and Rayner, 1920) in *Psychology AS for OCR*, p.235–6.

What research methods are used in the behaviourist perspective?

The main research methods used by behaviourist psychologists are the experiment and observations.

(1) The most frequently used method in behaviourist psychology is the experiment. This is because behaviourist psychologists aimed to apply the scientific method to the study of human behaviour.

> ## Core Study Example
>
> **Bandura, Ross and Ross (1961).** Bandura *et al.* developed behaviourism to incorporate social learning. This theory suggests that people do not necessarily learn only through direct experience but that they can also learn through observation and imitation. Bandura *et al.*'s study investigated the effect on young children of witnessing aggressive acts modelled by an adult on an inflatable doll (a Bobo doll).

(2) Behaviourist psychologists also use the observational method, as they believe that only observable behaviours can be studied scientifically.

> ## Core Study Example
>
> **Bandura, Ross and Ross (1961)** used a structured observation within their experimental study. **Milgram** observed participants reactions to thinking they were harming another person by administering shocks.

Table 1.6 Strengths and weaknesses of the behaviourist perspective

Strengths of the behaviourist perspective	Weaknesses of the behaviourist perspective
The behaviourist perspective applies the principles of the scientific method to the study of human behaviour.	The behaviourist perspective is limited to observable behaviours and therefore does not provide insights into internal mental processes.
Example:	Example:
The behaviourist perspective provides valuable insights into the effects of experience on cognition, including the development of dysfunctional cognitions such as phobias.	The behaviourist perspective is determinist. If all behaviour is conditioned, there is no room for free will in explaining human behaviour.
Example:	Example:
The behaviourist perspective provides a useful framework for the treatment of a range of psychological disorders.	The behaviourist perspective is reductionist. This means that it reduces the complexity of human behaviour to a set of stimulus–response relationships.
Example:	Example:

NB: Gaps have been left for you to identify Core Studies that are examples of behaviourist–perspective studies that show the strengths and weaknesses described above. When you have studied the relevant Core Studies, try to fill in these gaps.

1.7 Psychodynamic perspective

Psychodynamic psychology is one of the most enduring psychological approaches as it dates back to Freud but is still used in the training of clinical psychologists and therapists.

Some key assumptions of the psychodynamic perspective
- That all behaviours are shaped by unconscious desires and fears
- That behaviour is driven by internal factors rather than external/environmental factors.

What do psychodynamic psychologists study?

Psychodynamic psychologists attempt to study the internal workings of the mind and particularly the effects of unconscious desires on behaviour. Two of the studies that you meet in studying for AS examination G542: Core Studies can be described as psychodynamic. They are **Freud (1909)** and **Thigpen and Cleckley (1954)**. Freud analysed the development of a phobia in a small boy (Little Hans) while Thigpen and Cleckley described the history of a patient whom they diagnosed as having Multiple Personality Disorder.

What research methods are used in psychodynamic psychology?

(1) Psychodynamic psychology is based essentially on self-report.

> **Core Study Example**
>
> **Freud (1909)** and **Thigpen and Cleckley (1954).** Freud met Little Hans twice but based his analysis mainly on reports from Hans's father of what Hans himself said about his feelings and dreams. Thigpen and Cleckley interviewed their patient (Eve White) about her feelings and experiences.

(2) Psychodynamic psychologists may use the observational method in order to gain greater insight into the mind of their patient.

> **Core Study Example**
>
> **Freud (1909)** and **Thigpen and Cleckley (1954).** Freud observed Hans on one occasion at a birthday party. He also relied on Hans's father's observations of his son's behaviour. Thigpen and Cleckley observed how Eve behaved differently when she reported feeling in her different persona.

(3) Psychodynamic psychologists do not use the experimental method and are concerned with the importance of subjective feelings rather than objective data.

> **Core Study Example**
>
> **Freud (1909).** Freud in the study of Little Hans argued in favour of a subjective rather than an objective approach to data collection.

Table 1.7 Strengths and weaknesses of the psychodynamic perspective

Strengths of the psychodynamic perspective	Weaknesses of the psychodynamic perspective
The interview method enables the collection of rich, in-depth data.	Findings cannot be subjected to scientific scrutiny.
Example:	Example:
The focus on the individual enables the researcher to gain in-depth understanding of that individual.	The emphasis on the individual inevitably leads to small sample size, which means that findings cannot be generalised.
Example:	Example:
The psychodynamic approach enables the researcher to gain insight into internal processes that were not deemed suitable for study by behaviourist psychologists.	Data collection is subjective rather than objective and the therapist/researcher could plant ideas in the mind of the participant.
Example:	Example:

NB: Gaps have been left for you to identify Core Studies that are examples of psychodynamic–perspective studies that show the strengths and weaknesses described above. When you have studied all three of the psychodynamic–perspective Core Studies, try to fill in these gaps.

Summary

In this chapter we have discussed the five approaches and two perspectives that are studied at AS level and have indicated which research methods are used in the different approaches. In the next chapter we will explore in more depth the research methods that you need to be familiar with for G541: Psychological Investigations.

2.1 The experimental method

Psychology has for over a century regarded itself as a science. This means that the empirical evidence on which psychologists base their conclusions is generally collected according to the rules of scientific enquiry. The scientific method is based upon deduction. This means that scientists come up with theories and then they carry out investigations in order to obtain objective data that disprove or support their theories.

2.1 The experimental method	17
2.2 The observational method	28
2.3 Self-report	36
2.4 Correlation	40
Answers	44

Extend Your Understanding

Why do scientists try to disprove rather than prove their theories?

Imagine that you have a theory that boys run faster than girls. You ask a pair of children to run a race against each other, one boy against one girl. Every time you do this on ten occasions the boy wins. You might think that you should be able to claim that you have proved your theory. But scientists argue that you can never prove a theory completely because you never know what new evidence is waiting around the corner. You think you should give it one more go and on the eleventh occasion the girl wins. You have disproved your own theory. You cannot state categorically that boys run faster than girls because you have one piece of evidence that challenges the theory.

It is the scientist's job to come up with a new theory that, again, she or he should seek to disprove. If lots of people keep trying to disprove the same theory and no one comes up with evidence against it, we can then say that to date the theory appears to be supported by empirical research.

Key features of the experimental method

Experiments should all obey the same set of rules:

- **Theory:** The aim of an experiment is to test a hypothesis (predictions) with the aim of disproving or supporting it.
- **Test:** In order to test the prediction, it has to be established that one variable (thing) has a measurable effect on another variable (thing).
- **Control:** The study must be conducted under controlled conditions so that the researcher can identify that the effect that has been found is due only to an identified variable and not to other factors that were not tested.
- **Replication:** In order for support for a theory to be retested it is vital that any experiment can be replicated (imitated with the same results) by others. This means that the method must be identified precisely and be standardised so that it can be imitated. If the experiment is copied by others with the same or similar results then we say that it has been replicated.

Key steps in an experiment

- The experimenter comes up with a hypothesis.
- The experimenter designs an experiment to test that hypothesis.

- The experimenter manipulates one factor (the independent variable (IV)) that s/he has identified in his hypothesis as being likely to cause a particular effect.
- The experimenter measures the effect of this manipulation, and the factor that is measured is called the dependent variable (DV).
- Other variables are controlled.
- The experimenter analyses the difference in the mean results obtained in each condition.
- If a significant difference is found between means, this supports the alternate (experimental) hypothesis. If no significant difference is found, the null hypothesis is retained.

NB: You will note that one of the key features of an experiment is *not* that it is conducted in a laboratory. Although we refer to some experiments as 'laboratory experiments', this is because the researcher controls all the variables – it does not refer to where the experiment takes place. However, in order to control participant variables a laboratory experiment is normally conducted in a closed space like a laboratory, a classroom or a lecture theatre rather than a public place.

2.1.1 Null and alternate hypotheses

As explained above, when conducting an experiment the researcher will begin by formulating a prediction or hypothesis. This is the alternate or experimental hypothesis.

The null hypothesis is formulated as follows:
    That there will be no effect of X (the IV) on Y (the DV).
The alternate hypothesis is formulated as follows:
    That there will be an effect of X (the IV) on Y (the DV).

Extend Your Understanding

Null and alternate hypotheses – Core Studies example

Samuel and Bryant (1984) in their study of conservation ability in children formulated several alternate hypotheses. One of their alternate hypotheses was as follows:

That there will be an effect of asking one question instead of the standard two questions in Piaget's conservation task.

The null hypothesis was as follows:

That there will be no effect of asking one question instead of the standard two in Piaget's conservation task.

Q If you have already covered Samuel and Bryant's study, can you remember their other alternate hypotheses? (See p.44 for the answer).

For more information on alternate and null hypotheses, see Chapter 3, section 3.3, p.56.

2.1.2 Manipulation of the IV

In a true experiment the researcher manipulates the IV and in this way creates the different conditions of the experiment.

For a fuller discussion of independent variables, see Chapter 3, section 3.4, p.58.

Core Study Example

Manipulation of the IV

In **Loftus and Palmer** in the first experiment (see Table 2.1) the independent variable was the verb in the critical question. There were five different conditions of the experiment because there were five different versions of the questionnaire, each containing one of the following verbs: smashed, collided, hit, bumped and contacted.

Table 2.1 Independent variables in the Core Studies

	Examples of independent variables in the Core Studies
Loftus and Palmer 1	● The verb in the critical question
Samuel and Bryant	● Asking two questions (before and after the transformation) or one question (after the transformation only) of the participants ● Materials (water, Play-Doh, counters)
Bandura *et al.*	● Whether the children saw an aggressive model, a non-aggressive model or no model. ● Sex of the model
Piliavin *et al.*	● Whether the 'victim' was black or white ● Whether the 'victim' pretended to be ill or drunk ● Intervention of a model helper early or late, and in critical or adjacent areas

2.1.3 Measure of the DV

The DV is whatever the researcher has chosen to measure as a consequence of the manipulation of the IV. Generally, the DV is a numerical factor, which enables comparisons to be made between the results of different groups by calculation of group averages (usually means).

Extend Your Understanding

Comparing means

Three different types of averages can be calculated: mean, median and mode. The **mean** of a set of scores is calculated by adding all the scores and dividing by the number of scores. The **mode** is the most frequently occurring score in a set of scores. The **median** is calculated by ranking all the scores in order and determining the middle-ranking score. The **mean** is the most frequently used average in psychology research. Means are compared using tests of statistical significance.

See Chapter 3, section 3.7 on p.73 for more information on descriptive statistics. You do not need to know about how to calculate whether the difference between means is statistically significant until A2. This is discussed in Chapter 4, p.107–9.

Core Study Example

Measuring the DV

In **Loftus and Palmer** (experiment 1) the participants in each condition were asked to recall what speed they estimated the vehicles were travelling at when the collision occurred. Recalled estimated speeds in each condition were summed and means calculated. The mean estimated speeds in the different conditions were as shown in Table 2.2.

Table 2.2 Mean estimated speeds from Loftus and Palmer, Experiment 1

Verb in the critical question	Mean speed estimate in mph
Smashed	40.8
Collided	30.3
Bumped	38.1
Hit	34.0
Contacted	31.8

Table 2.3 Dependent variables in the Core Studies

	Examples of dependent variables in the Core Studies
Loftus and Palmer 1	● Estimated recalled speed
Samuel and Bryant	● Mean number of errors made in the conservation task
Bandura *et al.*	● Frequency of imitative aggressive acts ● Frequency of non-imitative acts ● Frequency of verbally aggressive behaviours
Piliavin *et al.*	● Latency (time lapse) between staged collapse of 'victim' and first helping intervention ● Number of passengers who left the critical area in response to the staged collapse of 'victim' ● In cases in which no-one intervened to help before the intervention of the model, latency (time lapse) between helping intervention of model and helping intervention from a participant

2.1.4 Control of variables

As explored above, when running an experiment your aim is to establish the effects of one thing (the IV) on another (the DV) (see Table 2.3). However, other things may interfere with your results, reducing reliability and validity. These other things are called extraneous variables or confounding variables.

For more information on variables, see Chapter 3, section 3.4, p.58.

Extend Your Understanding
Reliability and validity

Reliability means that the measure and the results are consistent. If your measure is reliable when you run your experiment several times you should obtain consistent results.

Validity means that your study is examining what you aimed to examine. For a study to be valid the results must also be reliable.

For a fuller discussion of the issues of reliability and validity, see Chapter 3, section 3.2, p.51.

Core Study Example
Control of variables

In **Bandura** *et al.* the nursery children were matched on ratings of aggression. However, the age range was 3–5 years and the children were not matched on age. In theory, age could have been a confounding variable. If all the older children ended up in the same group, for example, this might have affected the results.

Q When you have completed the following Core Studies in class, fill in the blanks in Table 2.4.

Answers are given at the end of this chapter, p.44.

Table 2.4 Control of variables in the Core Studies

	Well-controlled variables	Possible confounding variables
Loftus and Palmer	Task variables were well controlled as all participants watched the same _____ _____.	_____ may have been a confounding variable as it was not controlled for.
Samuel and Bryant	Task variables were well controlled as all the children were tested using the same _____.	_____ may have been a confounding variable as it was not controlled for.
Bandura *et al.*	____ _____ were well controlled as the children were all given the same toys to choose from in the experimental room.	The children were not matched on ___ so this may have been a confounding variable.
Piliavin *et al.*	Procedure was well controlled as the experiment was conducted in the same _____ _____ on the same route and the 'victim' collapsed after the same lapse of time.	_____ _____ were not controlled as the experimenters did not control who entered the carriage. However, the very large sample should ensure that this was not an issue.

2.1.5 Core Study examples that use the experimental method

- **Loftus and Palmer (1974)** *(Cognitive)*
- **Samuel and Bryant (1984)** *(Developmental)*
- **Bandura, Ross and Ross (1961)** *(Developmental)*
- **Piliavin, Rodin and Piliavin (1969)** *(Social)*

Piliavin, Rodin and Piliavin (1969) is a field experiment because it was conducted in a public place (the New York subway), hence participant variables were not controlled. The others are classed as laboratory experiments, although not one of them was conducted in a laboratory. **Loftus and Palmer (1974)** took place in a university in the United States; **Samuel and Bryant (1983)** in primary schools in Devon, and **Bandura, Ross and Ross (1961)** in a university nursery (Stamford, California). They are defined as laboratory experiments because they have an IV and DV and both participant and task variables are controlled.

Extend Your Understanding

Fuzzy areas in psychology

Did you expect to find some other examples of Core Studies that you can class as experiments? You may already have realised that not many issues in psychology are clear cut – there are lots of grey areas or fuzzy lines. There are other Core Studies that can be classed 'experiments', but there are reasons why they do not fit completely the above key features of an experiment and because of this the author prefers to class them as 'quasi-experiments'. However, you or your teacher may not agree with this. In psychology there are not always black and white answers. The definition of a quasi-experiment is that it uses some aspects of the experimental method but not all of them.

Core Study examples that might be classed as quasi-experiments

- **Baron–Cohen** *et al.* **(1997)** *(Cognitive)*
- **Dement and Kleitman (1957)** *(Physiological)*
- **Maguire** *et al.* **(2000)** *(Physiological)*
- **Milgram (1963)** *(Social)*
- **Reicher and Haslam (2006)** *(Social)*
- **Griffiths (1994)** *(Independent differences)*

The most common reason why experiments are classed 'quasi' is when the researcher has not manipulated an IV but instead has selected two groups for comparison that differ in one important feature (a naturally occurring or pre-occurring difference). This may be gender or age of participants, but there are other possibilities as well.

In **Baron–Cohen** *et al.* **(1997)** there was no manipulated IV. Instead Baron–Cohen *et al.* compared the performance of three groups with natural differences on a task. The groups were participants with two different clinical conditions (autism, Tourette's syndrome) and a sample of healthy (normal) participants.

In **Maguire** *et al.* **(2000)** there was no manipulated IV. The groups were taxi drivers and non-taxi drivers.

In **Griffiths** *et al.* **(1994)** there was no manipulated IV. The groups were gamblers and non-gamblers.

In **Dement and Kleitman (1957)** there was an independent variable (REM/NREM sleep). Thus this study could be described as a repeated measures experiment (see below) in which participants were woken during REM sleep and NREM sleep and the mean number of recalled dreams was compared in the two conditions. However, although the experimenter controlled when he woke the participants, he could not control the IV (REM/NREM sleep) and it is more properly termed a quasi-experiment or a case study.

In **Milgram (1963)** there was no independent variable. All participants underwent the same procedure. Therefore, although this study took place in a laboratory, it is a quasi-experiment rather than an experiment.

Reicher and Haslam (2006) has an experimental structure in that the researchers randomly allocated to groups, having matched participants on several variables, and they also manipulated several IVs (e.g. legitimacy). However, it was almost impossible to determine whether perceived changes in behaviour were the direct consequences of the manipulation of the IVs. This might be termed either a quasi-experiment or an experimental case study as it examined the behaviour of a group of individuals in depth over a period of several days.

2.1.6 Strengths and weaknesses of experiments

Table 2.5 Strengths and weaknesses of the experimental method

Research method	Strengths	Weaknesses
Experiment	Experiments enable you to test hypotheses by manipulation of an independent variable.	Experiments are often low in ecological validity as they are generally controlled situations removed from real life.
	Experiments are scientific as they follow standardised procedures, which enables replication.	Experiments are difficult to organise in practical terms as you have to run them in controlled conditions and this means sample sizes are usually small, thus reducing generalisability.
	Experiments enable the researcher to control extraneous variables, thereby improving reliability of results.	Participating in experiments, especially if run in laboratories, may cause anxiety or stress in participants (particularly children or vulnerable adults), and this is a problem in terms of ethics.
	Experiments normally produce quantitative data that can be subjected to statistical analysis, which ensures that results of different groups of participants can be meaningfully compared.	Experiments do not normally involve collection of qualitative data such as people's feelings as they participate, which means that the results are generally reduced to numerical data such as scores.

Identifying strengths and weaknesses of using an experiment in relation to stimulus material

In G541: Psychological Investigations you will be given an outline of a research project and be asked to comment on the strengths and weaknesses of using an experiment to collect your data. Here is an example.

Researchers conducted an experiment in a local shop investigating whether receiving the comment 'Have a good day' from the cashier increased the rating of how friendly the customer rated shop staff. As customers left the till after paying, to some customers the cashier said 'Have a good day' and to other customers the cashier said nothing. Outside the shop customers were asked to rate friendliness of the shop staff on a scale of 1 ('not very friendly') to 10 ('extremely friendly').

Q Outline one strength and one weakness of using the experimental method in this study. (6 marks)

A A strength of using the experimental method in this study is that it enables you to identify the effect of the independent variable (whether the cashier wished the customer a good day) on the dependent variable (how friendly the customer rated shop staff) using a controlled procedure. A weakness of using the experimental method in this study is that in a real-life situation such as a shop it is not possible to control all the variables so that you do not know how staff related to the customer in that shop before they purchased their goods at the till.

Here is another example. See whether you can identify one strength and one weakness in it yourself this time. (6 marks)

Q A psychologist has conducted an experiment to investigate whether the chewing of gum influences concentration. She recorded how many mistakes were made by children when answering questions about a passage they had read while chewing gum as compared with the number of mistakes made by children answering questions on a passage they had read while not chewing gum.

(a) A strength of using the experimental method in this study is...
(b) A weakness is ...

Likely responses will be found at the end of the chapter on p.44.

2.1.7 Experimental design

There are three main experimental designs:

(a) Independent measures
(b) Repeated measures
(c) Matched participants.

(a) Independent measures

In an independent–measures design participants are randomly allocated to groups and each group is tested in one condition.

Extend Your Understanding

Random allocation to groups

Before conducting an independent-measures experiment the experimenter puts the names of all participants into a hat and draws out names, allocating them in turn to conditions A and B.

Core Study Example

An independent-measures design experiment

Loftus and Palmer (1974) used an independent-measures design in their study of recall of speed of vehicles involved in a car crash (Experiment 1).

- The IV was the verb in the critical question.
- There were five conditions – smashed, collided, hit, bumped, contacted.
- Participants were randomly allocated to each condition.
- The DV was the mean estimated recall of speed at which the cars were travelling.
- Mean estimated speed was calculated in each condition and the difference in means was calculated.
- Loftus and Palmer found that there was a significant difference between recalled estimate of speed in the 'smashed' condition (40.8 mph) in comparison with the 'contacted' condition (31.8 mph).

(b) Repeated measures

In a repeated–measures design the same participants are tested in two or more conditions. The means obtained in each condition are then calculated and mean difference between conditions is calculated. If a significant difference is found, this supports the experimental hypothesis. If no significant difference is found, the null hypothesis is retained.

Core Study Example

A repeated-measures design experiment

None of the Core Studies used a pure repeated-measures design but **Samuel and Bryant (1984)** included one element of repeated measures. In this study, children's ability to conserve was measured. The independent-measures element was that the children were randomly allocated to the one question or the two question condition. The repeated-measures element was that each child repeated the experiment with three different materials: water, Play-Doh and counters.

- The IV was the nature of the material on which each child was tested.
- There were three conditions – volume (water), mass (Play-Doh) and number (counters).
- Participants were tested in all three conditions.
- The DV was the mean number of errors made by the children in each condition.
- The difference in mean number of errors was calculated and Samuel and Bryant found that there were significantly fewer errors made by the children in the number condition than in the volume or mass conditions.

(c) Matched participants

In a matched–participants design, participants are divided into groups on the basis of matching on one or more criteria such as age, gender, verbal ability, etc.

Core Study Example

A matched-participants design experiment

Bandura, Ross and Ross (1961) used a matched-participants design in their study of imitation of aggression in nursery-aged children.

- The children were matched on aggression ratings made in advance of the experiment.
- There were three conditions, so the participants were matched into trios and then one member of each trio was allocated to each condition.
- The three conditions were: aggressive model, non-aggressive model and a control condition of no model.
- The DV was mean observed frequency of imitative aggressive behaviours.
- Bandura, Ross and Ross found that the children in the aggressive model condition engaged in a higher mean frequency of imitative acts than children in the other conditions.
- The validity of this finding was increased because of the fact that the researchers used a matched-participants design – the children had been matched on aggression ratings prior to the experiment.

2.1.8 Choosing a design for your experiment: evaluation of the different designs

One experimental design is not better than another. However, one design is usually better suited to a particular investigation than another. When choosing an experimental design you need to evaluate what each offers in the context of your study. Table 2.6 outlines the main strengths and weaknesses of each design, but these should be considered only in the light of particular studies.

Table 2.6 Evaluation of different types of experimental design

	Strengths	Weaknesses
Independent measures	● No order effects as participants participate in the experiment once only ● Demand characteristics are reduced as the participants participate in the experiment once only	● Even with random allocation of participants to groups it is not possible to control participant variables effectively because sample size is normally small.
Repeated measures	● Removes participant variables as each participant is tested in both/all conditions	● Order effects need to be controlled. ● There is less control of task variables as different materials need to be presented each time in order to remove order effects. ● There is a greater likelihood of demand characteristics because participants go through the procedure more than once.
Matched participants	● Extraneous variables are well controlled	● It is impossible to control all extraneous variables so in practice participants are normally matched on only one or two variables.

See Chapter 3 for an explanation of the following terms:

● quantitative data
● order effects
● demand characteristics
● participant variables
● task variables.

2.1.9 Identifying strengths and weaknesses of different experimental designs in relation to stimulus material

In G541: Psychological Investigations you will be given an outline of a research project, which will state which experimental design has been used. You may be asked to comment on the strengths and weaknesses of the design chosen. Here is an example.

A researcher wants to conduct an experiment to investigate whether there is a difference in the concentration of secondary school students in the morning compared with the afternoon. Each student will be assessed in both the morning and the afternoon. This was a repeated-measures design.

Q Outline one strength and one weakness of using a repeated-measures design in this experiment. (6 marks)

A One strength of using a repeated-measures design is that participant variables are controlled as the same participants are tested in both conditions. This should enable the researcher to identify the effect of the IV (time of day) on the DV (student concentration). One weakness of using a repeated-measures design is that there is less control of task variables. You need to use a different test of concentration in order to avoid practice effects, which increases the possibility of the result being affected by the comparative difficulty of the two concentration tests.

Here is another example. See whether you can identify one strength and one weakness in it yourself this time.

A researcher has conducted an experiment to see if children recall more words from a list of common words when they learn and recall in the same classroom than if they learn in one classroom and recall in a different classroom. This was an independent-measures design.

Q Outline one strength and one weakness of using an independent-measures design in this experiment. (6 marks)

See the end of the chapter, p.44 for likely answers.

Extend Your Understanding

Order effects, practice effects and boredom effects

In a repeated measures design there are factors that need to be considered that might affect the reliability of the results. These include order effects, practice effects and boredom effects.

Order effects – When participants are asked to undertake the same or a very similar task in two conditions (for example, in the morning and the afternoon), the order in which the tasks are presented may affect the results. For example, if participants are given two different word lists to memorise in the morning and the afternoon and they remember more words correctly in the morning, this may be as a result of the manipulation of the IV (morning/afternoon) or it might be because the morning list is easier than the afternoon list. The order of presentation of the lists is therefore important. It is best if you can counter order effects by giving half the children one list (list A) in the morning and half the other list (list B) in the morning and then swapping round.

Practice effects – Practice effects can operate in a similar way to order effects. If you give children two word lists to memorise in the morning and the afternoon they may do better in the afternoon simply because the first time was like a practice and so results would be affected by their level of expertise. Practice effects are more difficult to control for than order effects. Again you can counterbalance by having half the children do the task first in the morning and half do the task first in the afternoon and swapping round, but this means that it will take two days to complete the study rather than one.

Boredom effects – Boredom is a factor that could operate in the opposite direction to practice effects. If children are given word lists in both the morning and the afternoon they may try their best in the morning, but they may be bored the second time around and not try so hard. If you use the same method as suggested for practice effects it should be possible to control for boredom effects as well as practice effects.

2.2 The observational method

The observational method is one of the most important data-collection methods available to psychologists. A key assumption of the scientific method discussed earlier is that only observable findings can be measured. The behaviourist perspective was developed a century ago and its chief exponents held to the fundamental principle of scientific research that only directly observable behaviours can be studied scientifically. As psychology developed as a discipline the understanding of what constitutes scientific research broadened. Psychologists now attempt to study mental processes that cannot be observed through normal observational methods. Nevertheless, an element of observation still plays a part in much research in psychology, even if it is not usually the principal method of data collection in many studies. Observation is perhaps of particular value to social psychologists as their aim is to study human interactions and group behaviours, which are normally observable.

Key features of the observational method

- In an observation, data are collected by someone observing (watching) participants and recording (taking notes of) what the participants do and say.
- Sometimes the observer is present and sometimes the observer is hidden behind a one-way mirror (a window that looks like a mirror from the participants' viewpoint).
- Other recording techniques can be used, including video recordings and CCTV footage.
- Observations may be conducted on their own or they may be conducted as part of an experiment.

Extend Your Understanding

Fuzzy areas in psychology

Although you need to keep separate in your mind experiments and observations (as these are classed as two different research methods for the purposes of G541: Psychological Investigations), it is important to realise that the two methods are not mutually exclusive. Experimenters normally observe participants during experiments for a variety of reasons, but there are also some experiments in which the data are actually collected using observational methods. Remember that what identifies an investigation as an experiment is whether it has an IV and a DV rather than where it is conducted or the details of the procedure.

2.2.1 Observation in the Core Studies

There is not one example of a Core Study in which the research method is observation alone. However, there are several examples of Core Studies that are experiments, quasi-experiments or case studies that involve an element of observation in their procedure. In fact, it is harder to think of a Core Study that does not involve any observation than one that does! Remember, when we discuss observations in the context of studies we are discussing observations made by the experimenters, not observations made by participants during the study. Have a look at Table 2.7 and you may be surprised at the extent to which observation constitutes part of the procedure in many of the Core Studies. One way to think about this is to consider whether the data could have been collected in the absence of the researcher or without a recording watched afterwards by the researcher. If you have not yet studied many of the Core Studies, you may need to return to this table at a later date.

Table 2.7 Observation in the Core Studies

Study	Approach	Observation	Role of observation in study
Loftus and Palmer	Cognitive	x	No observation
Baron-Cohen *et al.*	Cognitive	x	No observation
Savage-Rumbaugh *et al.*	Cognitive	√	Indoors: No observation needed as Kanzi's utterances were recorded directly by a computer attached to the lexigram Outdoors: Observer recorded (noted down) all Kanzi's utterances
Samuel and Bryant	Developmental	√	The researcher tested children on conservation tasks by recording each child's responses to the questions asked.
Bandura *et al.*	Developmental	√	Observation was the key data-collection method in this experiment. An observer coded and recorded each child's behaviour after seeing the aggressive/non-aggressive model (or not seeing a model – the control condition).
Freud	Developmental	√	Little Hans's father observed and made notes about Han's behaviour and what he said about his dreams and feelings.
Dement and Kleitman	Physiological	√	The researcher had to observe the EEG recordings in order to know when to wake up participants according to the schedule for each participant, e.g. alternately in REM sleep and NREM sleep.
Sperry	Physiological	√	The only data-collection method in this study was the researcher's observations of the responses made by the participants when asked to identify verbally or by touch stimuli presented to them.
Maguire	Physiological	x	No observation
Piliavin *et al.*	Social	√	Observation was the key data-collection method in this study. Observers in the subway carriage noted down how long it took for passengers to help a 'victim' and other details such as the race and gender of passengers in the carriage.
Milgram	Social	√	Observation was a key element in this study. There was an objective method of data collection (the recorded shock level each participant believed they had delivered). However, the researcher also noted down details of how the participants responded to the demands of the task, e.g. what they said, whether they looked stressed, etc.
Reicher and Haslam	Social	√	The key data method in this study was observation. It was as if the participants were in a kind of goldfish bowl (the simulated prison environment) as all their behaviour and conversations were observed and video-recorded.
Rosenhan	Individual Differences	√	This study included the collection by the pseudopatients of observational data concerning interactions between themselves and hospital staff.
Thigpen and Cleckley	Individual differences	√	This study was based on therapy sessions conducted by the researchers on a patient (Eve White). The therapists observed and noted down the patient's behaviour and responses to their questions.
Griffiths	Individual differences	√	The researcher observed and recorded the participants' gambling pattern and wins/losses at a fruit machine as well as their verbal reactions to their play in the Thinking Aloud condition (recorded on a tape recorder).

2.2.2 Different types of observation

As can be seen from the above examples, observation plays a variety of roles in different studies. Observations can be used to collect both **quantitative** and **qualitative** data and there are several different types of observation:

(a) Controlled observations
(b) Natural observations
(c) Participant observations.

(a) Controlled observations

These are conducted in a controlled environment such as a laboratory or classroom and are generally part of an experimental procedure. There is control over participants (the researcher has selected the participants and allocated them to conditions) and the participants have particular tasks to do.

> **Core Study Example**
>
> In **Bandura** *et al.* children were allocated to three conditions – aggressive model, non-aggressive model or no model condition. The researcher sat behind a one-way mirror and recorded the children's production in a controlled environment of aggressive acts after exposure to the model.

(b) Natural observations

These are conducted in a natural environment in which the experimenter has no control over who participates or what the participants do.

> **Core Study Example**
>
> **Piliavin** *et al.* is the closest of the Core Studies to an example of a natural observation. It was conducted in a natural environment (a subway carriage) and the researchers had no control over who got into the subway carriage and thus no control over the behaviour of the passengers. However, it was not completely natural because the researchers manipulated behaviour by introducing a 'victim' and then observing participants' reactions to the situation.

(c) Participant observations

This is really a type of natural observation, with the difference being that the observer takes an active role by becoming a fully participating member of the group being observed.

> **Core Study Example**
>
> There is no example of this among the Core Studies. The closest that we come to participant observation is when in some trials conducted by **Piliavin** *et al.* a model intervened to help the 'victim' after a certain amount of time had passed and the observers then recorded the impact of this confederate's actions on the naive participants.

> **Extend Your Understanding**
>
> **Understanding terms**
>
> A **confederate (or stooge)** is someone who participates in a study on behalf of the experimenter and who acts to shape or manipulate the behaviour of the other participants who are **naive** to the study and to the double role of the confederate.
>
> Being **naive** to a study means that you have not been told of its real purpose.

Overt/Covert observations

Just to complicate matters there are other dimensions of observations that you need to be aware of. Observations may be either **overt** (open) or **covert** (conducted in secret).

(a) Overt observations

Any observation conducted by the experimenter when the participant knows they are being observed is described as overt.

> **Core Study Example**
>
> In **Griffiths**, the participants were well aware that Griffiths was standing near them making notes of their gambling pattern and their wins/losses, so this was an **overt** observation.

(b) Covert observations

Any observation, controlled or natural, in which the participants are not aware that they are being observed is a **covert** observation.

> **Core Study Example**
>
> Here we have two very different examples of **covert** observations. In **Bandura et al.**, the observer used a one-way mirror so that the children would not be aware that their actions were being observed. However, the effect of the covert nature was slightly reduced by the fact that an experimenter stayed in the room with each child as some of them were clearly upset by this stage of the study. This meant that the children were aware of an adult presence despite the covert nature of the observation. In contrast, in **Piliavin et al.** two observers got into the subway carriage, pretending to be regular passengers, and then covertly made notes of what they observed.

Structured/unstructured observations

There is yet another important dimension of observations that you need to know about for Psychological Investigations. This is the way in which an observation is conducted or structured.

(a) Unstructured observations

In an unstructured observation the observer simply notes down anything and everything that they observe or that they think is important. This can be descriptions of participants' behaviour, conversations or how the participants appear to be feeling, or their reactions to events.

> **Core Study Example**
>
> In **Milgram** the researcher who was present in the room with the participant wrote down in an unstructured manner the participant's behavioural responses to the task they had been given. He sometimes recorded what they said or the fact that they seemed anxious or that they were sweating.

(b) Structured observations

In a structured observation the researcher operates with a predetermined observation schedule and a predetermined list of categories in order to facilitate analysis. There are two types of observation schedule:

(a) Time sampling
(b) Event sampling.

In **time sampling** the observer decides in advance not only the duration of the observation but also the subdivisions of the duration into time points or intervals. They then record what they observe at each time point/during each interval. This can be what a participant is doing on the minute every minute, for example, or it can be what the participant is doing during each minute interval. For this type of observation a stop–watch is necessary.

> **Core Study Example**
>
> In **Bandura *et al.*** the investigator chose to use **time sampling**. He noted down what each child was doing at 5-second intervals during a 20-minute observation, giving a total of 240 possible recorded behaviours.

Time sampling is particularly useful when investigating behaviours of uncertain duration. For example, if you are monitoring phone usage it is more useful to know at how many time points a person was on the phone during a time interval of, say, 20 minutes than simply that they made one phone call.

In **event sampling** the observer has a predetermined list of behaviour categories and they keep a tally by noting down each time a behaviour occurs.

> **Core Study Example**
>
> Among the Core Studies there is no example of a typical event-sampling observation in which the investigator notes down the frequency of several different behaviours during a set time period. **Bandura *et al.*** could have used this method, in which case instead of noting down what the child was doing every five seconds they would instead have recorded each time the child engaged in one of the predetermined list of imitative/non-imitative aggressive acts.

Other Core Studies that used a type of structured event-sampling method are **Savage-Rumbaugh *et al.*** and **Griffiths**, but in both these studies the investigators were interested in collecting data relating only to one type of behaviour. **Savage-Rumbaugh** and colleagues accompanied Kanzi when he was outdoors in the forest environment. They did not record everything that Kanzi did, but they recorded each time Kanzi made an utterance, and they judged whether it was correct and whether it was imitation, spontaneous utterance or prompted utterance. Similarly, **Griffiths** recorded how much time each participant stayed on a fruit machine, the total number of gambles they made and how many wins and losses they clocked up.

Event sampling is more practical than time sampling if there are several participants under observation and is more useful if the aim of the study is to assess frequency of particular events.

2.2.3 Strengths and weaknesses of the observational method

Table 2.8 Strengths and weaknesses of the observational method

Research method	Strengths	Weaknesses
Observation	Observations are often high in ecological validity as they are generally conducted in naturalistic environments.	Observations do not enable you to assess cause and effect unless they are part of a controlled experiment.
	Observations normally produce rich data. They may produce quantitative data that can be subjected to statistical analysis, but they can also produce qualitative data that can give some insight into people's reactions and feelings in relation to particular events.	Observations are often covert, which raises ethical issues as participants are not aware that they are being observed or that they are taking part in an investigation. There is normally no opportunity either for informed consent or for debriefing.
	Observations are comparatively easy to run in practical terms as you do not need to advertise for participants or disturb participants from their day-to-day activities if they are run in a natural environment.	In observations it is generally not possible to control variables, which means that there is little standardisation and they can be hard to replicate.
	Observations are often low in demand characteristics as people are usually not aware they are being observed.	Overt observations are not subject to the same ethical issues as covert observations, but they raise the problem of demand characteristics as people will not behave normally if they know they are being watched.

2.2.4 Inter-observer reliability

One way of strengthening an observation is to ensure that there are always at least two observers. This is to make sure that the data collected are reliable. Both observers employ the same schedule and use the same categories to independently record their observations. After the observation is concluded the data from different observers are compared and a statistical test can be run to assess the level of concordance. The data are generally regarded as reliable if agreement is at least 0.8 (i.e. the observers have at least 80 per cent of their data in common).

Core Study Example

In **Bandura et al.** some of the observations were conducted by two observers, but for most of them there was just one observer, which lowers the reliability of the results.

2.2.5 Strengths and weaknesses of different types of observations

Which particular observational method should be employed in an investigation depends on several factors. The aim of the investigation is the main factor, but other factors include the environment in which the observation will take place, the number of expected participants, the number of different behaviours that will be recorded and the nature of those behaviours. Each method has its own strengths and weaknesses and these should also be taken into account when designing an observation.

Q See whether you can fill in the blanks in Table 2.9 (answers are at the end of this chapter, p.45).

Table 2.9 Key strengths and weaknesses of different types of observations

Observational method	Strengths	Weaknesses
Controlled observation	In a controlled observation the variables are controlled, which enables the investigation to be _____ and in the context of an experiment may be able to show cause and effect.	Controlled observations are _____ in ecological validity as the participants are observed doing particular tasks, not engaging in normal behaviour.
Natural observation	Natural observations are high in _____ _____ as the participants are observed in normal behaviour.	Natural observations do not allow for _____ of variables.
Participant observation	Participant observation enables observers to engage in _____ observation in a natural situation.	Participant observation involves _____ as the participants do not realise that there are investigators in their midst.
Unstructured observation	Unstructured observations enable the investigator to collect rich _____ data.	With unstructured observations it can be easy to miss some things and also there is the possibility of observer _____.
Structured observation	Structured observations enable the investigator to collect _____ data that can be analysed statistically.	Structured observations rely on a list of _____ categories and the categories may not cover all the behaviours observed.
Time sampling	Time sampling gives good insight into how much of participants' _____ has been engaged in particular activities.	With time sampling it is difficult to be _____ if there are several participants under observation at the same time.
Event sampling	Event sampling enables _____ of different events to be recorded and compared.	Event sampling may not give the full picture if an event is tallied once but has a _____ duration.
Overt observation	Overt observation is _____ sound because it does not involve deception.	Overt observation is likely to be affected by _____ _____.
Covert observation	Covert observation is not likely to be affected by _____ characteristics as people are unaware that they are being observed.	Covert observation raises ethical issues with regard to _____ as participants do not know they are being observed.

2.2.6 Identifying strengths and weaknesses of different observational methods in relation to stimulus material

In G541: Psychological Investigations you may be given an outline of a research project employing the observational method. You may be asked to comment on the strengths and weaknesses of observations generally or you may be asked to comment on the strengths and weaknesses of the particular observational method used in the stimulus material presented. Here is an example.

Researchers want to conduct an observation investigating students' use of laptops in their free time in college.

Q Explain the difference between time sampling and event sampling in observational research. (4 marks)

NB: The above question does not ask you to refer in your answer to the study outlined.

A In time sampling the duration of an investigation is subdivided in a schedule of time points (e.g. on the minute every minute) or time intervals (e.g. during each five-second interval) and behaviours recorded that occur at those points or during those intervals.

In event sampling a predetermined list of categories of behaviour is drawn up and each time one of those behaviours occurs it is tallied, giving the frequency with which that behaviour occurs for the duration of the investigation.

Q Outline one strength and one weakness of conducting observational research in this study. (6 marks)

NB: This time you *are* required to contextualise your answer by referring to the stimulus material outlined.

A A strength of using an observation to investigate use of laptops in students' free time in college is that it is a method that is high in ecological validity as the observation would be conducted in the students' natural environment (e.g. a social area or cafeteria) and if the observation was covert the students would not be aware that their use of laptops was being observed.

A weakness of using an observation into use of laptops in students' free time is that while the observer will be able to use time sampling or event sampling to establish frequency of laptop use, there is a limit to the information that can be gained through observation. The observers will probably not be able to observe every screen in order to determine exactly what the students are doing on their laptops, e.g. sending emails, studying or playing internet games.

NB: Note that in each answer the two parts are clearly separated. This is good practice as it allows the marker to see clearly that you have answered both parts of the question.

Here is another example. See whether you can answer the questions yourself this time. (Likely answers will be found at the end of this chapter, p.45.)

Researchers want to conduct a covert observation in a self-clear works cafeteria investigating whether the employees clear up after they have finished their meal.

Q 1. Explain the difference between covert and overt observations. (4 marks)
NB: The above question does not ask you to refer in your answer to the study outlined.

Q 2. Outline one strength and one weakness of conducting a covert observation in this study. (6 marks)

NB: This time you are required to contextualise your answer by referring to the stimulus material outlined.

2.3 Self-report

Self-report is a method of data collection in which the participant themselves answer questions about their behaviour, thoughts or feelings. Questions may be asked in an interview or in the form of a questionnaire that participants are asked to respond to.

Key features of the self-report method

- Instead of using an objective method of data collection, participants are asked to make subjective judgements.
- Interviews are a commonly used technique in clinical psychology and psychotherapy. They can be structured, semi–structured or unstructured.
- Usually self-report questions are responded to by participants themselves, although occasionally others respond for them, e.g. in the case of small children or people with learning difficulties who are unable to respond on their own behalf.
- The most common form of self-report in psychological investigations is the questionnaire or psychological measure.
- As with observations, self-report is a method in its own right, but it is also frequently incorporated into experiments.

Table 2.10 Self-report in the Core Studies

Study	Approach		Role of self-report in study
Loftus and Palmer	Cognitive	√	Participants responded to a questionnaire about their memory of the car crashes they had seen on video.
Baron-Cohen *et al.*	Cognitive	√	Participants responded to the mental states portrayed in the eyes of photographed faces by selecting the appropriate adjective to describe each mental state.
Savage-Rumbaugh *et al.*	Cognitive	x	No self-report
Samuel and Bryant	Developmental	x	No self-report
Bandura *et al.*	Developmental	x	No self-report
Freud	Developmental	√	Freud interviewed Hans on one occasion. Otherwise the data-collection method was second-hand self-report as Hans's father reported to Freud Hans's dreams and feelings.
Dement and Kleitman	Physiological	√	The participants reported their dreams into a tape recorder and on occasions responded to questions from the investigator.
Sperry	Physiological	x	No self-report. Participants were not asked to report their own experiences of how they had been affected by the brain disconnection operation.
Maguire	Physiological	x	No self-report
Piliavin *et al.*	Social	x	No self-report
Milgram	Social	x	No self-report
Reicher and Haslam	Social	√	Participants responded to daily psychometric tests, including a self-report measure of depression.

Table 2.10 continued

Study	Approach		Role of self-report in study
Rosenhan	Individual differences	√	In Rosenhan's follow-up study, hospital staff were asked to rate on a ten-point scale the likelihood that patients attending for psychiatric treatments were pseudopatients. This is a form of self-report.
Thigpen and Cleckley	Individual differences	√	This study was based on interviews with the patient (Eve White) that constituted therapy sessions conducted by the investigators.
Griffiths	Individual differences	√	There was a self-report element in this investigation as one group of participants were asked to voice aloud their reactions and feelings as they gambled (Thinking Aloud condition) and these data were recorded onto tape.

2.3.1 Interviews

There are three different types of interview:

(a) Unstructured
(b) Structured
(c) Semi-structured.

(a) Unstructured interview

In an unstructured interview there is no predetermined structure to the interview, although the interviewer will normally have some goal or sense of direction in mind. The interviewer asks open-ended questions and the answers given by the interviewee stimulate new questions. The directed but unstructured interview is the type of interview normally used in a therapeutic context as the therapist's aim will be to enable the patient to talk about whatever is troubling them.

(b) Structured interview

In a structured interview the interviewer has a predetermined list of questions which they stick to. Respondents are all asked the same questions in the same order.

There are no examples of structured interviews in the Core Studies.

> **Core Study Example**
>
> In **Thigpen and Cleckley** Eve White was interviewed on several occasions by the investigators, who gave direction to the sessions but also responded to the different personalities the patient exhibited.

(c) Semi-structured interview

In a semi-structured interview the interviewer has a list of questions but the approach is flexible and can be shaped by the interviewee's responses.

There are no examples of the use of structured or semi-structured interviews in the Core Studies.

2.3.2 Questionnaires and other psychological measures

- Questionnaires and psychological tests such as personality tests and IQ tests are all self–report measures.
- Questions in a questionnaire can be open or closed.
- Open questions are open ended and allow free rein in answering them.
- Closed questions have a limited number of possible responses. They can be questions that require a simple yes/no answer or they can require an answer from a range of possible answers.
- Questionnaires frequently use a rating scale. They can consist of questions or statements that participants respond to on a scale (e.g. a Likert scale) where responses may take the form of 'strongly disagree' to 'strongly agree' on a scale of 1–4 where 1 = strongly disagree and 4 = strongly agree.
- If participants have to select answers from a range of possible responses they can be referred to as forced–choice questions.

Table 2.11 Questionnaire use in the Core Studies

Core Study	Questionnaire purpose	Question type
Loftus and Palmer	To allow participants to answer questions concerning the video clips they had watched	A mixture of open-ended and closed questions
Baron-Cohen *et al.*	To gauge participants' reading of mental states in the eyes of photographed faces	Forced choice of adjectives
Reicher and Haslam	Self-rating depression scale	Closed questions (rating scale)
Rosenhan	Questionnaire assessing psychiatrists' confidence in their diagnosis of patients as mentally ill or pseudopatients	Rating scale

Table 2.12 Strengths and weaknesses of self-report

Research method	Strengths	Weaknesses
Self-report	Self-report is a valuable method of investigating thoughts and feelings that cannot be investigated using other methods.	Self-report is a subjective method of data collection that is not subject to scientific scrutiny.
	Self-report is a practical research method that enables investigators to collect large quantities of data quickly when the questionnaire method is used.	Interviewing can be time-consuming and is not normally conducted on large samples.
	Self-report measures are usually standardised and easily reproduced, enabling studies to be replicated.	It is not possible to gauge whether respondents are telling the truth in their responses.
	Self-report data can produce numerical data that can be analysed using statistical methods.	If self-report responses require respondents to recall events or feelings, their responses can be affected by reliability issues.

Table 2.13 Strengths and weaknesses of different types of self-report methods

Self-report method	Strengths	Weaknesses
Unstructured interview	Unstructured interviews allow collection of rich, qualitative data.	Unstructured interviews make it hard to compare the responses of one interviewee with those of another.
Structured/semi-structured interview	Structured interviews enable comparisons to be made between the responses of different interviewees.	Structured interviews may limit interviewees' responses so that full information is not received.
Open-ended questions	Open-ended questions enable respondents freedom to answer as they choose.	Open-ended questions make the collection of quantitative data and statistical analysis difficult.
Closed questions	Closed questions enable collection of quantitative data and therefore make statistical analysis possible.	Closed questions may limit respondents' choices so that full information is not received.

NB: The strengths and weaknesses of unstructured interviews and open-ended questions are similar, as are the strengths and weaknesses of structured interviews and questionnaires that use closed questions.

2.3.3 Identifying strengths and weaknesses of self-report methods in relation to stimulus material

In G541: Psychological Investigations you may be given an outline of a research project based on self-report. You may be asked to comment on the strengths and weaknesses of self-report generally or you may be asked to comment on the strengths and weaknesses of the particular self-report method used in the stimulus material presented. Here is an example.

Researchers conducted an investigation about dreaming using a self-report questionnaire consisting of closed questions. Some examples of what participants were asked are presented below:

- How often do you recall your dreams? (Never/sometimes/always)
- How often to do you recall having nightmares? (Never/sometimes/always)
- Do you remember what people say in your dreams? (Never/Sometimes/Always)

Q Outline one strength and one weakness of using closed questions in this study. (6 marks)

A Closed questions allow quantitative data to be collected and analysed. A strength of using closed questions in this study is that they enable the researcher to find the mean number of times people say they remember their dreams and the mean number of times that people recall having nightmares.

A weakness of using closed questions is that they do not allow you to find out all the possible answers that people might come up with. For example, the question 'How often do you recall your dream?' does not allow participants to express more detail such as whether they have clear memories or only vague memories of their dreams. Also, closed questions do not allow the respondent to go into details with regard to dream content.

Now try answering the following questions yourself. (Possible answers can be found at the end of the chapter, p.46.)

A researcher wants to use a self-report questionnaire to finding out why psychology under-graduate students at a popular university chose to study psychology.

Q 1. Suggest one open and one closed question that could be used to investigate subject choice. (4 marks)

Q 2. Discuss the validity of the closed question you have suggested to investigate subject choice. (4 marks)

2.4 Correlation

Correlation differs from the previous research methods in that it is not a method of data collection but a data-analysis technique. It is used in studies that are not experimental, i.e. cause and effect cannot be established. It enables relationships between variables to be established but not cause and effect.

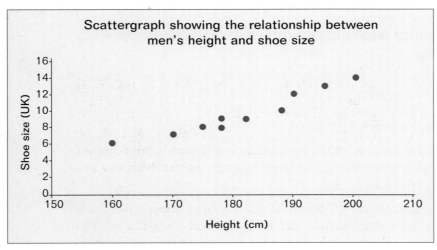

Figure 2.1

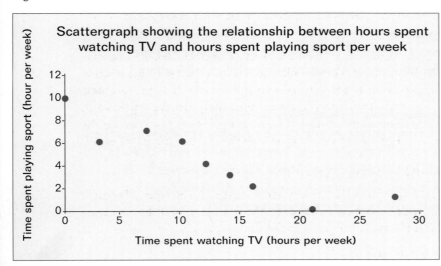

Figure 2.2

Key features of correlations

- Correlation is a data-analysis technique, not a method of data collection.
- Correlations are relationships between variables.
- Correlations can be positive or negative.
- When a correlation is positive, the values of one variable increase as the values of the other variable increase.
- When a correlation is negative the values of one variable decrease as the values of the other variable increase.
- Correlations are shown by drawing scattergraphs that show the relationship between participants' scores/measurements on both variables.

What conclusions can we draw from the correlation shown in Figure 2.1? Can we say that being tall causes people to have bigger feet? No. Can we conclude that having bigger feet causes people to be tall? No. All that we can conclude is that the two variables are related. We can never draw conclusions about cause and effect, even when a strong relationship can be seen between two variables, as we have not manipulated an independent variable.

What conclusions can be drawn from the correlation shown in Figure 2.2? Can we say that spending time watching television prevents people from playing sport? No. Can we say that spending time playing sport prevents people from watching television? No. All we can say is that there is a relationship between the two variables and that it is in a negative direction.

2.4.1 Correlations in the Core Studies

There is only one example of correlation as a key technique in the Core Studies. This is the result reported in **Maguire et al.**, in which the relationship between period of time spent as a taxi driver and the extent of difference in hippocampal

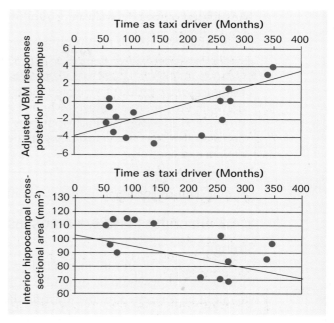

Figure 2.3

volume of taxi drivers as compared with normal controls is analysed. This is an important result as it suggests that the brain is plastic. This is because it shows that taxi drivers who have been driving a long time appear to have greater differences in the posterior and anterior hippocampus compared with normal controls than taxi drivers with less experience. One of the correlations is in a positive direction and the other in a negative direction. The posterior hippocampus showed an increase in volume in taxi drivers while the anterior hippocampus showed a decrease in volume in taxi drivers. (See Figure 2.3.)

These correlations are particularly seductive and it is very hard to resist the conclusion that cause and effect has been established. However, the same rule applies as in the above examples. The researchers did not manipulate an independent variable, so cause and effect cannot be established. It looks likely that the brain changes as a result of experience, but this has not been proven. It is possible that people with less volume in the anterior hippocampus and greater volume in the posterior hippocampus make for better taxi drivers and are more likely to stick with the job.

There are two other examples of correlational analysis used in the Core Studies. In one case correlation was performed to ensure reliability and in the other to ensure validity. In **Bandura et al.** two observers both recorded the aggressive behaviours of a number of the children and their results were correlated to check for reliability (inter-observer reliability). In the other case, **Baron-Cohen et al.** correlated the results on their 'reading the mind in the eyes' test with results on Happé's strange stories task to establish the validity of the new test as a test of theory of mind.

2.4.2 Alternate and null hypotheses in correlations

In a study that uses the correlational rather than the experimental method, the researcher may still begin by formulating a prediction or hypothesis. However, this is framed in different terms from an experimental hypothesis. It is always formulated in the following way:

That there will be a relationship between X and Y.

The null hypothesis is formulated as follows:

That there will be no relationship between X and Y.

> ### Core Study Example
>
> **Maguire *et al.* (2000)** formulated the hypothesis that there would be a relationship between time spent as a taxi driver and extent of difference in hippocampal volume of taxi drivers and controls. The null hypothesis in this case was that there would be no correlation between time spent as a taxi driver and extent of difference in hippocampal volume in taxi drivers and controls.

For more information on alternate and null hypotheses, see Chapter 3, section 3.3, p.56.

2.4.3 Strengths and weaknesses of correlational analysis

Strengths

Correlation is a useful tool in psychology as it allows us to measure the relationship between variables which it would be difficult or unethical to manipulate experimentally. For example, we might be interested in investigating the relationship between reported stress and ill health. It would be impractical and unethical to manipulate stress or health. However, it is possible to correlate self-reported levels of stress with health data in order to establish whether there is a relationship between the two.

As can be seen from the examples cited above of use of correlation in **Bandura *et al*.** and **Baron-Cohen *et al*.**, it is also a useful tool for establishing reliability and validity.

Weaknesses

As already discussed, the major problem with correlational evidence is that correlation does not imply causation. In other words, just because two variables are correlated does not mean that one of them has caused the other to change.

2.4.4 Interpreting scattergraphs in relation to stimulus material

In G541: Psychological Investigations you may be presented with a scattergraph and be asked to draw conclusions from the data presented. Here is an example.

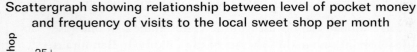

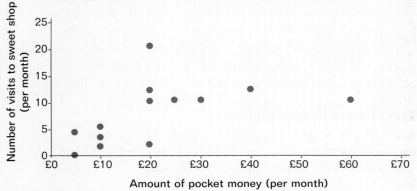

Researchers have conducted an investigation into the relationship between the amount of weekly pocket money children are given and the number of times they visit the local sweet shop to buy sweets.

Q Outline two conclusions that can be drawn from this scattergraph. (5 marks)

See the end of this chapter on p.46 for a possible answer.

Figure 2.4

2.4.5 Drawing scattergraphs from correlational data

In G541: Psychological Investigations you may be presented with a table of data and be asked to draw a scattergraph. Here is an example.

Researchers investigated, using a self-report measure, hours spent watching television and weight in kilograms in eight-year-old boys.

Table 2.14 Correlation between weight of eight-year-old boys and hours spent watching TV

Participant	Hours spent watching TV per week	Weight in kilos
1	12	25
2	15	30
3	12	20
4	20	32
5	8	25
6	8	30
7	14	28
8	10	22
9	6	25
10	18	34

Q 1. Sketch an appropriately labeled scattergraph displaying the results. (4 marks)

(For an answer see the example scattergraph at the end of chapter, p.47.)

Q 2. Outline one conclusion that can be drawn from the scattergraph you have drawn. (3 marks)

(See end of the chapter, p.47, for a likely answer.)

Answers

2.1.1 Null and alternate hypotheses
That there will be an effect of age on ability to conserve.
That there will be an effect of material on ability to conserve.

2.1.4 Control of variables

Table 2.4 Answers Control of variables in the Core Studies

	Well-controlled variables	Possible confounding variables
Loftus and Palmer	Task variables were well controlled as all participants watched the same **video clips**.	**Gender (or age)** may have been a confounding variable as it was not controlled for.
Samuel and Bryant	Task variables were well controlled as all the children were tested using the same **materials**.	**Intelligence (or gender)** may have been a confounding variable as it was not controlled for.
Bandura *et al.*	**Task variables** were well controlled as the children were all given the same toys to choose from in the experimental room.	The children were not matched on **age** so this may have been a confounding variable.
Piliavin *et al.*	Procedure was well controlled as the experiment was conducted in the same **subway carriage** on the same route and the 'victim' collapsed after the same lapse of time.	**Participant variables** were not controlled as the experimenters did not control who entered the carriage. However, the very large sample should ensure that this was not an issue.

2.1.6 Strengths and weaknesses of experiments
One strength: Likely answers will include the fact that you have an IV and DV so can establish cause and effect; control of variables; provides numerical data that can be analysed to compare means; controlled procedure so can be replicated.

One weakness: Likely answers will include low ecological validity (test effect putting children off); unsuitable test material as may test reading ability instead of concentration; confounding/extraneous variable is reading ability.

2.1.9 Identifying strengths and weaknesses of different experimental designs in relation to stimulus material
One weakness: Likely answers will include participant variables (one group of pupils may have better memories than the other).

One strength: Likely answers will be that there will be no order effects or boredom effects.

2.2.5 Strengths and weaknesses of different types of observations

Table 2.9 Answers Key strengths and weaknesses of different types of observations

Observational method	Strengths	Weaknesses
Controlled observation	The variables are controlled, which enables the investigation to be **replicated** and in the context of an experiment may be able to show cause and effect.	Controlled observations are **low** in ecological validity as the participants are observed doing particular tasks, not engaging in normal behaviour.
Natural observation	Natural observations are high in **ecological validity** as the participants are observed in normal behaviour.	Natural observations do not allow for **control** of variables.
Participant observation	Participant observation enables observers to engage in **covert** observation in a natural situation.	Participant observation involves **deception** as the participants do not realise that there are investigators in their midst.
Unstructured observation	Unstructured observations enable the investigator to collect rich **qualitative** data.	With unstructured observations it can be easy to miss some things and also there is the possibility of observer **bias**.
Structured observation	Structured observations enable the investigator to collect **quantitative** data that can be analysed statistically.	Structured observations rely on a list of **predetermined** categories and the categories may not cover all the behaviours observed.
Time sampling	Time sampling gives good insight into how much of participants' **time** has been engaged in particular activities.	With time sampling it is difficult to be **accurate** if there are several participants under observation at the same time.
Event sampling	Event sampling enables **frequencies** of different events to be recorded and compared.	Event sampling may not give the full picture if an event is tallied once but has a **long** duration.
Overt observation	Overt observation is **ethically** sound because it does not involve deception.	Overt observation is likely to be affected by **demand characteristics**.
Covert observation	Covert observation is not likely to be affected by **demand characteristics** as people are unaware that they are being observed.	Covert observation raises ethical issues with regard to **deception** as participants do not know they are being observed.

2.2.6 Identifying strengths and weaknesses of different observational methods in relation to stimulus material

Answers are likely to be as follows:

A1. A covert observation is one in which the observer(s) are hidden or are under cover and the participants do not realise that their behaviour is being observed.

A2. A strength of using a covert observation in a study of whether employees clear up after they have eaten in their self-clear cafeteria is that if the employees do not realise they are being observed they will behave in their normal way, ensuring that demand characteristics do not affect the results and thus ensuring higher reliability of findings.

A weakness of using a covert observation in a study of employee behaviour in a works cafeteria is that it is ethically unsound as the employees have not been forewarned that they are the subject of a study and they could feel upset if they find out later that they were being watched without their consent.

Remember, to gain full marks you need to explain the terms you use and for question 2 you have to clearly identify the strengths and weaknesses in the context of a self-clear works cafeteria.

2.3.3 Identifying strengths and weaknesses of self-report methods in relation to stimulus material

A1. One open question that could be used to investigate subject choice is: 'What was your main reason for choosing to study psychology at university?'

One closed question that could be used to investigate subject choice is: 'How important were career motives in your decision to choose psychology at university on a scale of 1–4 where 1 = not at all important, 2 = not very important, 3 = quite important, 4 = very important?

A2. A question in a questionnaire is valid if it helps the researcher answer his research question. The question I have suggested is valid because the answer would help the researcher find out the comparative importance of different factors in students' decision-making process with regard to choosing to study psychology at university.

2.4.4 Interpreting scattergraphs in relation to stimulus material
Conclusions that can be drawn are:

● Generally the higher the pocket money per month the greater the frequency of sweet shop visits (positive relationship).

● There is an outlier — one child who only received a relatively low amount (£20) of pocket money paid the most visits to the shop.

● Once pocket money has reached £20 per month there is a ceiling effect — that is those on really high pocket money (above £20) do not spend relative to their greater income.

2.4.5 Drawing scattergraphs from correlational data

A1.

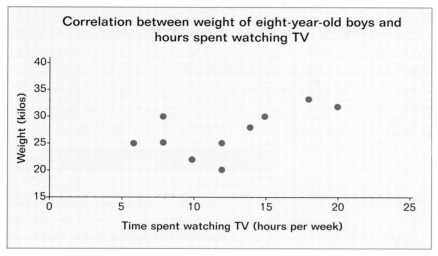

Figure 2.5

A2. One conclusion is that there is a positive correlation between the weight of eight-year-old boys and mean hours spent watching TV per week. The more TV boys self-reported watching, the greater their weight.

Note to students and teachers

Please bear in mind when using these sample questions and answers, that the answers are not designed to be perfect top–band answers. They are to point you in the right direction when you are thinking about how to answer questions in the exam, you will have to use your own knowledge and the guidance in this book, to reach for those top marks.

3 Issues in psychological investigations

3.1 Ethics   48
3.2 Reliability and validity   51
3.3 Hypotheses   56
3.4 Variables   58
3.5 Sampling   60
3.6 Procedures   65
3.7 Data analysis   73
Answers   80

3.1 Ethics

A top priority of researchers in any field that deals with human participants is to ensure that they conform to high ethical standards.

> **Extend Your Understanding**
>
> **Defining ethics**
>
> Ethics may be defined as a set of moral rules about human conduct. Such rules are heavily influenced by time (past/present) and by culture and religion.

As you may have realised if you have already studied some of the Core Studies (especially the social and developmental approach Core Studies), the ethical code by which British psychologists work today (*Code of Ethics and Conduct*, British Psychological Society, 2009) is much stricter than guidelines in the past. Think about each Core Study that you know and decide which ones did not follow a strict ethical code. Now try to recall the date at which those studies were published – or look them up if you can't remember. Are these two features of the studies related? You will probably find that those published longest ago are the most ethically problematic. If there is one that does not fit the pattern, it just might be **Savage-Rumbaugh's (1986)** study of language acquisition in bonobos. This is a relatively recently published study, but many of you may feel that bringing up bonobos in captivity and studying them intensively is unethical. The issue here is that psychologists currently abide by a far less strict ethical code with regard to animal participants than human participants.

For OCR AS Psychology the key ethical rules that you need to know and should apply in both evaluating studies and responding to source material in Psychological Investigations are as follows.

3.1.1 Avoidance of psychological harm

It is essential that any research conducted by psychologists and psychology students does not cause psychological harm to participants. This means that studies should avoid presenting participants with tasks or scenarios that might induce unpleasant emotions or states of mind such as anxiety, fear, stress, unhappiness, nor must they expose participants to any physical risk. Probably the Core Study that resulted in the highest degree of psychological harm is **Milgram (1963)**. If you have studied it, you will know why. If that is one you haven't come to yet, you may be in for a shock!

Of course, it is impossible to foresee every situation and it may happen that what appears to be a completely harmless study may cause such feelings in a few participants. For example, it is unlikely that you would class **Loftus and Palmer's (1974)** study of reconstruction of memory as an unethical study. But have you ever thought that it is quite likely that one of the many students in their sample may have experienced a bad car crash themselves or lost a family member in a car crash? Does that thought make you feel differently about their study? One way to avoid causing accidental psychological harm would have been to explain to participants before the study began that they would be seeing video footage of car crashes and that they need not go ahead if they thought they might find this upsetting. This should be done at the time that informed consent is obtained and is called offering the participants the right to withdraw. Loftus and Palmer may have informed their participants of the content of their experiment, but if they did, it is not detailed in their report. You may also have noticed that the older the study, the less likely it is to mention details such as how a sample was obtained, or whether ethical guidelines were followed.

3.1.2 Informed consent

The British Psychological Society guidelines require that, where practicable, researchers should always obtain informed consent from participants prior to starting. This means that participants should be given information about what they will be asked to do during the study and they should confirm verbally or in writing that they understand the study and are willing to participate. In the case of children, parental consent should be obtained in advance and the children themselves should be asked for their assent – that is to say, whether they are happy to continue. In practice, when researchers carry out studies in schools in the UK, the school normally informs parents in writing of the possibility that research may be carried out with their child, and asks them to inform the school if they wish their child to be withdrawn from any such research studies. Asking individuals to opt out rather than opt in ensures higher numbers of participants while still offering parents the right of informed consent.

> **Class Activity**
>
> Discuss whether you think that obtaining parental informed consent is a sufficient safeguard for the child? If you have already looked at the developmental-approach studies, you will know that Freud studies Little Hans with the willing consent of his father. Do you think that Hans was treated ethically by his father and Freud?

Q How many of the Core Studies explicitly refer to having obtained informed consent from participants? See Table 3.10 at the end of this chapter, p.80, for the answer.

3.1.3 Deception

Information given to participants (or the parents of child participants) does not have to include the exact aims of the investigation but at the same time it should not be deceptive.

Q Which of the Core Studies would you regard as having practiced deception? See Table 3.11 at the end of this chapter, p.81, for possible answers.

3.1.4 Right to withdraw

During the introduction to the study when informed consent is obtained the researcher must tell participants that they have the right to withdraw, and the right to not answer any question at any time. Particular attention should be given to ensuring that children understand that they can ask to stop at any time.

Q Which of the Core Studies reported offering participants the right to withdraw? Which of the Core Studies in practice made it difficult/impossible for participants to withdraw? See Table 3.12 at the end of this chapter, p.82, for answers.

3.1.5 Debrief

At the end of the study participants should be made aware of the real aims of the study and should be given the opportunity to ask questions of the researchers. This is called the debrief. During the debrief participants should be given the opportunity to ask for the results of the study if it is published and they should be informed that any discussion or publication of the study will ensure anonymity of participants.

Q Which of the Core Studies reported debriefing participants? In which of the Core Studies would debriefing have been impossible? See Table 3.13 at the end of this chapter, p.83, for answers.

3.1.6 Confidentiality/anonymity

Individual participants should not be identified or identifiable in any write-up of the study, nor should the participants discuss individuals' performance with anyone. This is to respect their privacy.

Q Which of the Core Studies broke the principle of anonymity? See the end of this chapter, p.83, for the answer.

3.1.7 Responses to ethics issues in source material

(a) Identifying ethics issues in source material

In the Psychological Investigations examination paper you will be given an outline of a research project and you might be asked to comment on ethical considerations in the study as outlined. Here is an example.

Researchers conducted an experiment in a local shop using covert observation to investigate whether a cashier's behaviour at the till affected customers' responses and behaviour. The cashier was a confederate and was asked to use in turn different behaviours, e.g. smiling, touching the customer on the arm, wishing them a good day, etc. Two observers noted the response of customers to these different behaviours.

Q Outline two ethical issue that this study raises.(4 marks)

A One ethical issue is that this observation was conducted covertly. This means that the participants were unaware that they were being observed and therefore informed consent was not obtained and participants were not debriefed. The other ethical issue is that one of the cashier behaviours was touching customers on the arm. This is a behaviour that might make some customers uncomfortable.

(b) Ways of dealing with ethical issues

You could also be asked how to deal with ethical issues raised in source material. If this is the case, as long as you know all the points of the ethical code discussed above it should be possible for you to suggest ways of dealing with ethical issues presented in source material. Let's take the same source material above and see how the ethical issues identified could be dealt with.

Q Outline how **one** of the ethical issues you have identified could have been dealt with. (2 marks)

A 1. It might have been possible to inform customers when they entered the shop that an observational study was being conducted in order to improve staff-customer relationships without pinpointing the precise focus of the study. This would have enabled the customers to withdraw if they did not want to be observed by not shopping in that particular shop that day.

A 2. The customers could have been stopped as they left the shop and fully debriefed.

A 3. It might have been better not to include 'touching the customer's arm' as one of the cashier behaviours as some people might find this intrusive.

Here is another example. See whether you can answer this yourself. Likely answers will be found at the end of this chapter, p.83.

Researchers want to conduct an observation investigating students' use of their free time in college. They conduct a covert observation in a campus coffee bar throughout the day.

Q 1. Outline two ethical issues that this study raises. (4 marks)

Q 2. How would you deal with one of the ethical issues raised in this study? (2 marks)

3.2 Reliability and validity

If we were to hold a vote on which concepts in A Level Psychology were the most confusing, surely reliability and validity would win hands down!

How would we hold this vote if we wanted to find out whether the above statement is true? If we took a random sample of psychology students at a large sixth-form college (pulling their names out of a hat) and asked them to rate how much they liked various concepts (e.g. reliability, validity, ecological validity, generalisability) in psychology on a scale of 1–4 (where 1 = not at all and 4 = very), what answer do you think we would obtain? Would our results be reliable and valid?

Can you spot the problem? Our measure was a clearly outlined reliable (consistent) scale, but our question (how much they liked various concepts) was not a valid measure of level of confusion! While it may be true that whether you like a concept is probably affected by how confusing you find it, the two could be quite different. We can say that the study lacked face validity (whether it does what it says on the tin). So the results would not allow us to draw valid conclusions about the relative confusion caused to students by the different concepts. The measure we chose was a reliable one. But our question did not ask what we intended it to ask. This would have meant, of course, that our study had low validity.

So we decide to run our study again. This time we ask the clear question: 'How confusing do you find the following concepts in psychology? Please respond on a scale of 1–4.'

Is our question valid this time? Yes – we are asking exactly what we want to know. Is our study therefore valid? Unfortunately not. Can you spot the problem? This time we did not clearly outline our measure. We asked students to respond on a scale of 1–4 but we did not state whether 1 = 'not at all confusing' or 'very confusing'. Some students would take 1 to equal 'not at all' while other students might take 1 to equal 'very'. This means that this time our measure would definitely not provide reliable results as there would be no internal consistency. Would our study still be valid as our question was a valid one? No. If your measure is not reliable this immediately invalidates your results.

So we have to run our study a third time. This time we have our valid question: 'How confusing do you find the following concepts in psychology?' We have also managed to produce a clear, reliable measure – 'Please respond on a scale of 1–4, where 1 = not at all confusing, 2 = not very confusing, 3 = quite confusing, 4 = very confusing'. Now we can rest assured that our study has produced results that are reliable and we can draw valid conclusions.

A measure is reliable if it produces consistent results. A study has face validity if it answers the question the experimenter wants answered (does what it says on the tin). If the measure used is also reliable then we can probably draw the conclusion that it is valid.

Hopefully the above explanation has reduced the confusion in your mind about these two different concepts. Just in case you are still confused, you will find highlighted below some examples of reliability and validity issues in the Core Studies.

3.2.1 Reliability and validity in the Core Studies

In **Dement and Kleitman's** study of sleep and dreaming, REM (rapid eye movement) sleep was measured by electrodes attached around the eyelids. This is an objective method of data collection that provides a **reliable** measure of eye movements during sleep, recorded by an EEG machine. Are we able to conclude that the EEG data are a valid measure of dreaming?

No – we cannot be sure that REM = dreaming. Therefore if the study had been based on EEG data alone we would not be able to conclude that the data provided a valid measure of dreaming. The self-report measure, meanwhile, appears to be a valid measure of dreaming, but is it reliable? Possibly not, because there is another variable that could get in the way of the results and that is memory. Sometimes people woken during REM sleep could not remember whether they had been dreaming. This does not prove that they had not been dreaming, merely that they could not remember whether they had. You might conclude from this that self-report of dreaming is not a very consistent (reliable) measure of dreaming, in which case you would have to conclude that **Dement and Kleitman's** study is not a completely valid study of dreaming.

Another example is **Piliavin** *et al.***'s** study of helping behaviour when observers measured the latency before subway passengers intervened to help an experimenter who was pretending to be ill or drunk. The observers provided a reliable measure of the latency before intervention using a stop-watch. However, this study was arguably not a valid test of the theory of 'diffusion of responsibility' – the theory that the more people that are in the vicinity of a crisis, the less likely the victim is to receive help. The reason that it may not be valid is that the bystanders were unable to get away completely from the crisis because they were travelling in a subway carriage. Given that the 'diffusion of responsibility' is based on the idea that people will shirk their responsibility and move away from the crisis, the very unusual situation of being contained in a small space reduces the validity of the study. Thus we can conclude that while the data collected were reliable, we cannot be sure that the study was a valid test of the theory of 'diffusion of responsibility'.

Here is a third example from the Core Studies. See whether you can work out the answers for yourself (answers are given at end of the chapter, p.84).

Samuel and Bryant tested children's ability to conserve following Piaget's model. With each child the experimenter carried out the same procedure (with the exception of the manipulation of the independent variable, which was asking one question or two – the standard Piagetian approach). The experimenter asked the following questions each time (dependent on which material he/she was presenting to the child):

Liquid: 'Do you think the amount of liquid in these glasses is the same or different?'

Mass: 'Do you think the amount of Play-Doh in these two shapes is the same or different?'

Number: 'Do you think the number of counters in these rows is the same or different?'

The experimenters noted down the children's replies and calculated the number of errors made by each child, then compared mean number of errors in each condition (the standard two-question condition or the one-question condition).

Q 1. Do you think this procedure will have provided data that reliably measure whether children's scores on the conservation tasks are affected by the number of questions asked each time? In other words, do you think that this procedure will produce consistent results?

Q 2. Do you think that the experiment as described appears to have face validity in terms of assessing the effect of asking one or two questions each time on the measurement of children's ability to conserve? In other words, do you think that it does what the experimenter wants it to do?

Q 3. Do you conclude that Samuel and Bryant's study is a valid study of how measuring children's ability to conserve is affected by the way in which they are asked the question (standard two-question or one-question condition)? In other words, do you think that the conclusions the experimenters have drawn are both reliable and valid?

3.2.2 Responses to questions of reliability/validity in source material

In the Psychological Investigations examination paper you will be given an outline of a research project and you may be asked to comment on the reliability/validity of the measure outlined. Here is an example.

Researchers wanted to conduct an experiment to investigate the ability of ten children aged six and ten children aged nine to identify basic emotions in faces. The participants were shown six photographs of the same person displaying in each case a different basic emotion (sadness, happiness, surprise, anger, disgust, fear). Each time the experimenter asked the following question: 'What do you think the person in the photograph is feeling?' One mark was recorded for each correct response, giving a total out of six.

Q Evaluate the reliability and validity of the way the dependent variable (DV) has been measured in this study. (10 marks)

To get full marks on this question you have to show that you understand the meaning of both the terms 'reliability' and 'validity' and that you explore the strengths and weaknesses of the measure of the DV in this study in terms of both reliability and validity.

You might begin by defining the terms, for example, reliability means consistency of the measure whereas validity in this context means whether the measure actually measures what the researchers want it to. Likely answers might include comments about the reliability of the measure, such as that the procedure was standardised in that the participants were all shown the same photographs and asked the same question, which should contribute towards reliability of the measure. However, the source material does not provide information about how a response is coded as correct – does the child have to say the word 'sadness' to be marked as correct or can they say things like 'she does not look very happy' to be marked correct? So while the procedure is standardised, the actual measure of the DV is probably not very consistent (reliable).

Likely answers with regard to validity will depend in part on the answer given with regard to reliability. If you have decided that the reliability of the measure is OK, then you state that and go on to discuss other aspects of validity, e.g. face validity, ecological validity. If, however, you have decided that the reliability of the measure is not good, you cannot conclude that the measure of the DV is valid. Whichever way you argue on reliability, to gain full marks you should also explore other aspects of validity. Likely answers on validity might include the fact that the faces were likely posed (by the same person) so the emotions will be stereotyped rather than real (low ecological validity), or that the photographs are stills whereas in real life faces are always moving, so emotion is not usually judged on the basis of one snapshot (low in ecological validity). So if you thought the measure of the DV was reliable you might conclude that although the measure was reliable, it was not particularly valid because it was low on ecological validity. If, however, you thought the measure of the DV was not reliable, you should conclude that the study was not valid on the grounds that it was both low in ecological validity and used a measure that was not reliable.

Here is another example. See whether you can answer this yourself. Likely answers will be found at the end of this chapter, p.84.

Researchers wanted to conduct a repeated measures experiment to investigate the ability of 20 primary school-aged children to concentrate on a task while music was playing and when they were required to do the same task in silence. The dependent variable (DV) was how many words the children remembered correctly from two different lists of ten words presented for them to look at for one minute, a) when music was playing and b) in silence. The children were asked to write down each time as many words as they could remember immediately after the list was taken away. The DV was the number of words remembered correctly out of a possible total of ten in each condition.

Q Evaluate the reliability and validity of the way the dependent variable (DV) has been measured in this study. (10 marks)

3.2.3 Ecological validity

When researchers conduct studies, one of their goals is to ensure that the way in which the research is conducted is as naturalistic (close to real-life situations/behaviour) as possible. When this is achieved, the study is described as being high in ecological validity. When the procedure is removed from real life, the study may be criticised for being low in ecological validity. Ecological validity is one aspect of overall validity.

Ecological validity in the Core Studies

An example of a Core Study that has high ecological validity is **Piliavin** *et al*. This was a field experiment conducted on the New York subway. It is high in ecological validity because it took place in a real subway carriage with real passengers. However, a limitation is that an undergraduate student staged a collapse (pretending to be ill or drunk) and we do not know how life-like their acting was! An example of a Core Study that is low in ecological validity is **Loftus and Palmer**. This was a laboratory experiment in which undergraduate students watched video clips of car accidents. This was an artificial situation and did not test how memory would be affected by questions asked afterwards in the emotional and potentially distressing situation of a real car accident.

Q When you have read the Core Studies, copy and complete the table below (Table 3.1). You should decide whether each study is high or low in ecological validity and then explain briefly your decision in the column entitled 'evidence'. There is not really one correct answer. The important thing is to provide evidence to support your judgment. However, if you turn to the end of this chapter, p.85 you will find likely responses.

Table 3.1 Ecological validity in the Core Studies

Study	High/Low in ecological validity	Evidence
Loftus and Palmer		
Baron-Cohen et al.		
Savage-Rumbaugh		
Samuel and Bryant		
Bandura et al.		
Freud		
Dement and Kleitman		
Sperry		
Maguire et al.		
Piliavin et al.		
Milgram		
Reicher and Haslam		
Rosenhan		
Thigpen and Cleckley		
Griffiths		

Ecological validity in source material

In the Psychological Investigations examination paper you will be given an outline of a research project and you might be asked to comment on the ecological validity of the investigation outlined. Here is an example.

University researchers want to conduct a study of the behaviour of sixth-form college students in their lunch hour. Two of the researchers station themselves in each of the four main areas of the cafeteria and record their observations using the time-sampling method (they record behaviours in their area every 20 seconds for 20 minutes).

Q Outline one issue relating to ecological validity in this investigation and discuss the possible effects of this on the validity of the study. (6 marks)

A Ecological validity can be defined as how close to real life a study is. One issue in this observation of students in their lunch hour is that the observers will be noticeably older than the college students and probably strangers. This might affect the behaviour of the college students. They may become aware that they are being watched (demand characteristics) and may modify their behaviour, for example they may behave differently from normal, e.g. being more polite and cautious so as not to offend the adults (social desirability effect).

Here is another example. See whether you can answer it yourself. (A likely response will be found at the end of the chapter, p.86).

Researchers want to investigate the effect of listening to pop music on student revision effectiveness. They run an independent-groups experiment in which 50 randomly selected A Level students are randomly allocated to one of two conditions. One group sits in a classroom revising set material for two hours while listening to loud pop music while the other group sits in another classroom revising the same set material for two hours in silence. The students then all sit the same multi-choice test and the DV is student score on the test out of 20.

Q Evaluate the ecological validity of the proposed investigation. (6 marks)

3.3 Hypotheses

Most researchers in psychology begin with a hypothesis (theory) that they want to test and then construct a study to test that hypothesis.

(a) Alternate or experimental hypotheses
In an experiment the alternate (experimental) hypothesis predicts the effect the independent variable will have on the dependent variable. In correlational studies the alternate hypothesis will predict a relationship between two variables (positive or negative).

Hypotheses can be either one-tailed or two-tailed.

- In a one-tailed hypothesis the direction of the effect or relationship is predicted.

- In a two-tailed hypothesis the direction of the effect or relationship is not predicted.

(b) The null hypothesis
The null hypothesis is really the starting point from which alternate hypotheses are developed (which explains the name 'alternate' for the experimental hypothesis – it is the alternative to the null). In an experiment the null hypothesis predicts no effect of the independent variable on the dependent variable. In a correlation the null hypothesis predicts no significant relationship (positive or negative) between variables.

(c) Operationalised hypotheses
This is a complicated term which means simply that the details of how your hypothesis will be tested are reported.

Let's look at some examples from the Core Studies.

3.3.1 Hypotheses in the Core Studies

In **Loftus and Palmer** the alternate hypothesis is that language will have an effect on memory for an event.

The null hypothesis is that there will be no effect of language on memory for an event.

The operationalised hypothesis is that when asked to recall estimated speed at which cars were travelling in a video clip of a car crash, the verb in the critical question will have an effect on participants' response.

This is a two-tailed hypothesis.

However, you could express this as a one-tailed hypothesis: that when asked to recall estimated speed at which cars were travelling in a video clip of a car crash, the stronger the verb used in the critical question, the higher will be the recalled estimated speed.

In **Baron-Cohen** *et al.* the alternate hypothesis was that individuals with high-functioning autism will be impaired on an advanced theory of mind task in comparison with people without autism or people with another clinical condition.

The null hypothesis is that there will be no effect of clinical condition (high-functioning autism) on ability in an advanced theory of mind task.

The operationalised hypothesis is that when asked to respond to a forced choice of adjectives describing the mental states conveyed in the eye region of photographed faces, people with high-functioning autism will be impaired on the task in comparison with control groups of normal people and people with Tourette's syndrome.

This is a one-tailed hypothesis as the direction of the difference has been predicted.

A two-tailed hypothesis would not be appropriate in this investigation.

3.3.2 Hypotheses in source material

In the Psychological Investigations examination paper you will be given an outline of a research project and you may be asked to identify or frame a null or alternate hypothesis relevant to the investigation outlined. Here is an example.

A researcher has investigated the effect of chewing gum in a concentration task. She has tested secondary school-aged children by giving them a page of text to read and asking them to spot spelling mistakes in the text. She has recorded the number of mistakes made by children chewing gum while doing the task as compared with those not chewing gum.

Q Suggest an appropriate alternate hypothesis for this experiment. (4 marks)

A An appropriate alternate hypothesis for this experiment is that there will be an effect of chewing gum on concentration of secondary school-aged children (two-directional).

Q Suggest an operationalised alternate hypothesis for this experiment. (6 marks)

A An operationalised two-tailed alternate hypothesis for this experiment is that when secondary school-aged children are tested in a concentration task involving spotting spelling mistakes in a page of text, there will be

> a difference in the number of mistakes found by those chewing gum during the task and those not chewing gum. An operationalised one-tailed alternate hypothesis for this experiment is that when secondary school-aged children are tested in a concentration task involving spotting spelling mistakes in a page of text, children chewing gum during the task will spot more mistakes than those not chewing gum.

Here is another example. See whether you can answer it yourself. (A likely response will be found at the end of the chapter, p.86.)

> A researcher has conducted a correlational study to investigate the relationship between the amount of exercise taken per week by female college students and their concern with their appearance as shown in a self-report measure. The first variable was 'self-rating of the importance of appearance' measured on a ten-point scale (where 1 = not important and 10 = extremely important). The second variable was 'amount of exercise taken in hours per week'.

 Suggest an appropriate null hypothesis for this study. (4 marks)

3.4 Variables

The term variable simply means factor, but in psychology you need to use the specific term 'variable' when discussing factors involved in shaping behaviour. Proving a causal relationship between variables means being able to show that one variable (variable A) is directly exerting an influence on another variable (variable B) and the relationship is not reciprocal (i.e. variable B does not exert an influence on variable A). If two variables are shown to be related to each other but you cannot prove the direction of influence, we say that the variables are correlated (related). Cognitive psychologists often apply correlational analysis if they have used a method other than an experiment to collect their data.

3.4.1 The independent and dependent variables

The independent variable (IV) is the variable manipulated by the experimenter.

An IV in a quasi-experiment is a natural or pre-occurring difference between groups that is the subject of the experiment (e.g. gender, or a clinical condition such as autism allows for comparisons with a control group without the condition).

The dependent variable (DV) is what is measured by the experimenter. This usually provides numerical data that can be analysed statistically.

See Chapter 2, 2.1.1, p.18 for more on IVs and DVs.

Operationalising the IV and the DV

As we have seen in 3.3.1 (above), when you are asked to operationalise the alternate hypothesis this simply means that you have to explain the hypothesis in the concrete terms of your study. The same applies to operationalising the IV and the DV.

For example, if you are intending to study people's memory in different conditions, your IV may be that participants will be given a memory test either a) in silence or b) with background noise.

Your operationalised IV will explain this in more detail.

For example: the IV will be that participants will be asked to perform a task while seated *either* in a silent classroom *or* while sitting in a noisy cafeteria at lunchtime. The two conditions of this study are 'doing the experimental task in a silent room' and 'doing the experimental task in a noisy area'.

In this same example the DV may be performance in a memory test.

The measure of the DV will explain how exactly 'performance in a memory test' will be measured in your study. For example, the DV will be total score out of 20 of words remembered correctly when participants are asked to recall as many words as possible from a list of 20 high-frequency words following a distractor task (reading a short passage).

3.4.2 Identifying and operationalising/measuring the IV and DV in source material

In the Psychological Investigations examination paper you will be given an outline of a research project and you may be asked how the independent variable was operationalised or how the dependent variable was measured in the investigation outlined. Here is an example.

A researcher has investigated the effect of noise on a concentration task. She has tested secondary school-aged children by giving them three minutes to read a page of text and asking them to circle deliberate spelling mistakes. She has recorded the number of mistakes (maximum of 12) spotted by children doing the task in silence as compared with those doing the task with loud music playing.

Q Identify the independent variable (IV) in this experiment. (2 marks)

A Silence/noise.

Q Explain how the IV was operationalised in this experiment. (4 marks)

A Secondary school children were asked to perform a task (spotting spelling mistakes in a page of text). The independent variable was that one group of children did this task in silent conditions for three minutes while the other group did the task while the experimenter played loud music for three minutes.

Q Identify the dependent variable in this experiment. (2 marks)

A Score on a concentration task.

Q Explain how the DV was measured in this experiment. (4 marks)

A The DV in this experiment was score on a concentration task. This was measured by counting the total number of deliberate spelling mistakes (maximum = 12) spotted and circled in a passage of text read by the children in each condition.

Here is another example. See if you can do this yourself. (A likely response will be found at the end of the chapter, p.86).

Researchers wanted to conduct an experiment to investigate the effect of training on the ability of 10 five-year-old children to identify basic emotions in faces. One group of participants (Group A) were trained before they undertook the task while the other group (Group B – the control group) were not. The training (conducted on the day before the experiment) consisted of the children listening to a story about emotions and being shown pictures of faces displaying the basic emotions discussed in the story. In the experiment stage, participants from both groups were individually shown six photographs of the same person displaying in each case a different basic emotion (sadness, happiness, surprise, anger, disgust, fear). Each time the experimenter then asked them the following question: 'What do you think the person in the photograph is feeling?' One mark was recorded for each correct response, giving a total out of six.

Q 1. Identify the independent variable in the experiment described above. (2 marks)

Q 2. Explain how the independent variable was operationalised. (4 marks)

Q 3. Identify the dependent variable (DV) in the above study. (2 marks)

Q 4. Explain how the DV was measured and results obtained in the above study. (6 marks)

3.4.3 Reliability and validity of measurement

Reliability and validity of measurement has been discussed above, section 3.2, p.51. Reliability of measurement is largely bound up with control of variables. If variables have not been well controlled, the reliability of your measure may be affected by extraneous variables.

Confounding and extraneous variables

Closely related to the issue of reliability and validity of measurement is the issue of extraneous and confounding variables. These are not quite synonymous (they mean almost but not quite the same thing), but for our purposes we can treat them as the same. We use the term 'confounding' as that expresses the idea that this other thing has messed up (confounded) our results. When we use the term 'extraneous' this conveys the idea that this other thing is one outside of our control and may have had some effect on the results without necessarily negating the results. In practice, both confounding and extraneous variable have the same effect – they reduce the reliability of our results and hence the validity of the study.

3.5 Sampling

Once a researcher has decided on the hypothesis that they wish to test and the design and procedure of their planned study, the next step is to obtain participants. This is referred to as obtaining the sample. The sample is the participants. There can be as few as one participant or as many as thousands in the sample. The sample can be composed of one, two or several different groups. You will probably have seen participants referred to as 'subjects' in some of the studies you have come across. Usually these are studies that were conducted some time ago and it is now regarded as more ethically sound to use the term 'participant'.

3.5.1 Types of sample

There are different ways in which researchers can obtain their sample. The method they choose is dependent on the nature and aim of the proposed study and practical concerns such as time constraints and whether characteristics of the sample (for example, gender or being diagnosed with a clinical condition) are part of the study or not. What are the smallest and largest examples you have come across so far in the Core Studies? The smallest sample in the Core Studies is one. Both **Freud** in his study of Little Hans and **Thigpen and Cleckley** in their study of Multiple Personality Disorder had a sample of one (although to Thigpen and Cleckley at times it must have seemed as though they were dealing with more than one person!).The largest sample size reported in the Core Studies is more than 4,000. That was the number of passengers on the New York subway that **Piliavin** *et al.* estimated had been participants in their field experiment on bystander behaviour.

Although there are several different ways in which participants can be obtained for a study, the three main ways that you need to know about at AS Level are:

(a) Opportunity sample
(b) Random sample
(c) Self-selected (volunteer) sample.

(a) Opportunity sample

An opportunity sample is one composed of participants who happen to be in the right place at the right time for your research. Although not highly regarded as a sampling method (because it is unlikely to be representative), this is probably the most common method that psychologists use to obtain a sample. This is because it is often the easiest way of obtaining participants and for some research (e.g. field experiments, some observations) it is the only way to obtain a sample. It can have some face validity. If, for example, your aim is to conduct a survey on attitudes towards supermarket shopping and you stand outside a large supermarket on a typical Saturday morning and ask everyone who comes out of the shop about their shopping experience, you will probably have a reasonably representative sample of attitudes. Or will you? Think about it. You are interviewing only those people who choose to shop at that supermarket. Probably those who don't like large supermarkets will not shop there. Their views will not be heard in your study. Also, is there anything special about Saturday shoppers?

Much psychological research that uses opportunity sampling is based on undergraduate psychology students who are always available to researchers and often have to participate in research for course credits. Unfortunately this means that much interesting research cannot be generalised beyond this population. Remember, even when you use an opportunity sample, informed consent should always be obtained prior to participation unless you are conducting a covert observation (see Chapter 2, p.31).

(b) Random sample

This is the method that is most highly regarded in psychology but is in practice rarely used. The aim of random sampling is that you gain a truly representative sample of participants from a particular population of interest. For example, if you are interested in feelings about A Level workload in your sixth-form college, the best way of sounding opinion is to enter all the names of students at your college into a hat (if it is a small college), or into a computer for random-number generation (if it is a large college), and randomly select a subset of the population (say, 5 per cent) as your sample. This is so that every student at the college has an equal chance of being picked for involvement in your study. The example just given is a manageable method of obtaining a sample, which is fine if you are interested only in your own college. But most psychologists are interested in behaviour and attitudes in much bigger populations. Let's rethink this project. How would a psychologist go about obtaining a random sample of all A Level students in the country to research the same question? Could this be done in practice? You can see the problems this would entail.

> **Q** How many of the Core Studies do you think used random sampling? What would you guess (or suggest from memory)? The answer to this question will be found at the end of this chapter in Table 3.3 on p.87.

Remember, even if you obtain your sample by a random method, every participant still has to give their informed consent. If you obtained a sample of 50 students from your college using a random-sampling method, but on further enquiry five students refused to participate, would your sample still be a genuinely random one? What about if ten or fifteen did not want to participate? You might think this would be OK, but once any of your sample withdraw, the random selection process begins to lose validity. You could end up interviewing, say, half of your sample who all stated that their A Level workload was manageable and you might then draw the conclusion that A Level students do not find A Level work too demanding. But if you subsequently interviewed those who had refused to participate, you might find that most of them had pulled out due to being too overloaded with A Level work to participate! So your apparently random sample would no longer be representative.

(c) Self-selecting (volunteer) sample

Self-selecting sampling is probably the second most commonly used method of obtaining a sample for psychology research after opportunity sampling. The difference between an opportunity sample and a self-selecting sample is that whereas in the former case the experimenter approaches a possible participant and asks them if they would be willing to participate in their study, in a self-selecting sample the experimenter simply publicises the study in appropriate places/ways and waits for people to put themselves forward as participants.

Obtaining such a sample can be done in many ways. Traditional methods are using posters and leaflets to advertise a project and ask for volunteers. However, where you place your publicity is an issue. If you advertise in a college or university, your volunteers will almost certainly be students. What happens if you want people of a range of ages, from other walks of life or with particular medical conditions? Other possible methods include approaching local firms, or GP surgeries (family doctors), and asking them to ask for volunteers from their workforce/patients. This enables a higher degree of targeting of the sort of population you are hoping to obtain volunteers from. Other methods are to advertise in newspapers and magazines or on local radio stations. A very common method nowadays to obtain a self-selected sample for a questionnaire study is to use the email system of large organisations. You could also use sites such as Facebook.

The main issue with self-selecting samples is the motivation of the participants for volunteering. It is usually because they have a particular interest in the focus of the project you are conducting. What effect do you think this will have on your data?

Table 3.2 Strengths and weaknesses of sampling methods

Sampling method	Strength	Weakness
Opportunity	Easy to obtain	Often not representative, though can be if large and carefully obtained
Random	The most representative sampling method	Very difficult to obtain unless the target population is limited
Self-selected	Ethically sound as all participants have volunteered	Very unlikely to be representative and difficult to obtain in large numbers

3.5.2 Sampling in the Core Studies

You may already have discussed in class the fact that not all the Core Studies identify their sampling method clearly by using the terms 'opportunity/random/self-selected' sample. This is frustrating for teachers and students alike as it makes it difficult to answer questions on the samples in Paper G542: Core Studies.

Q In Table 3.3 see whether you can identify which core studies state clearly their sampling method and which do not. Given the explanations provided above, see whether in the case of those that don't refer to sampling method you can determine which method they probably used. Likely answers will be found at the end of the chapter, p.87.

Table 3.3 Sampling method in the Core Studies

Core Study	Sampling method clearly identified (circle yes or no)	If stated, which method was used?	If not stated, which method do you think was used?
Loftus and Palmer	Yes/No		
Baron-Cohen et al.	Yes/No		
Savage-Rumbaugh	Yes/No		
Samuel and Bryant	Yes/No		
Bandura et al.	Yes/No		
Freud	Yes/No		
Dement and Kleitman	Yes/No		
Sperry	Yes/No		
Maguire et al.	Yes/No		
Piliavin et al.	Yes/No		
Milgram	Yes/No		
Reicher and Haslam	Yes/No		
Rosenhan	Yes/No		
Thigpen and Cleckley	Yes/No		
Griffiths	Yes/No		

3.5.3 Suggest/outline appropriate samples/sampling methods in source material

In the Psychological Investigations examination paper you will be given an outline of a research project and you may be asked to suggest an appropriate sampling method or to outline how you would obtain a sample for the project described. Here is an example.

Researchers wanted to conduct a repeated–measures experiment to investigate the ability of 20 primary school-aged children to concentrate on a task while music was playing and when they were required to do the same task in silence.

Q Suggest an appropriate sampling method that could be used in this study and explain your choice. (4 marks)

A An appropriate sampling method that could be used would be random sampling. This would entail getting a computer to generate 20 names randomly from a database containing all the names of children attending a local primary school. I would choose this method because every child would have an even chance of being picked and this should ensure that the sample is representative of the target population (the children at the school) and there would be no obvious biases in the selection process.

Here is another example. See if you can do this yourself. (Likely responses will be found at the end of the chapter, p.89.)

A researcher wants to conduct a correlational study to investigate the relationship between the amount of exercise taken per week by female college students and their concern with their appearance as shown in a self-report measure. The first variable was 'self-rating of the importance of appearance' measured on a ten-point scale (where 1 = not important and 10 = extremely important). The second variable was 'amount of exercise taken in hours per week'.

Q Suggest an appropriate sampling method that could be used in this study and explain your choice.

3.5.4 Identify strengths and weaknesses of sampling techniques described in source material

In the Psychological Investigations examination paper you will be given an outline of a research project and you may be asked to comment on the strengths and weaknesses of the sampling techniques described in the source material.

Researchers want to investigate the effect of listening to pop music on student revision effectiveness. They run an independent-groups experiment in which a self-selected sample was obtained by advertising in the sixth-form social centre of a college for A Level students who were asked to participate in the study during one lunchtime and were randomly allocated to one of two conditions.

Q Identify one strength and one weakness of the sample selection method outlined. (4 marks)

A One strength of the selection method outlined is that it is ethically sound because only self-selecting students were asked to participate, so pressure was not put on people who did not really want to be involved in the study. One weakness of the selection method outlined is that it may not be representative of students in general. For example, those who are willing to give up their lunchtime for a research project may be students who enjoy schoolwork and usually revise in a quiet atmosphere and this may bias the results.

Here is another example.

Researchers want to conduct a study on shopping patterns of families with young children. They use an opportunity sample. They attend several different mother and toddler sessions (music group, coffee session, etc.) held on different weekdays at a local church hall and interview the mothers about their shopping habits.

Q Identify one strength and one weakness of the sample selection method outlined. (4 marks)

A One strength of the selection method outlined is that it is easy and practical for the experimenter to reach their target population as they know that the people who attend such sessions will have young children. One weakness of the selection method outlined is that it will not be a representative sample of families with young children. It might be culturally biased as not all families from different ethnic communities would want to attend sessions in a church hall, or it would be biased against families in which both parents work full time and cannot attend toddler groups that run during the day.

Here is another example. See if you can do this yourself. (Likely responses will be found at the end of the chapter, p.89.)

Researchers want to conduct a study to assess suitability of two standardised literacy tests for primary school children in year 6. They ask four local schools if they will participate, each of which has two Year 6 classes of approximately 30 children in each. Two schools agree and contact parents to ask whether they are willing for their children to participate in research on literacy that involves doing two different literacy tests. As a result they obtain a self-selected sample of 30 children.

Q Identify one strength and one weakness of the sample selection method outlined. (4 marks)

3.6 Procedures

Extend Your Understanding

For G541, the term 'procedure' refers to all the steps that you take in designing and conducting an investigation. Normally in scientific papers the overall process is described as the method and the term 'procedure' is used to describe the task procedure, i.e. the steps taken once you have your investigators/participants ready to begin. For the purpose of the examination you are expected to include in answer to questions about 'procedure' details of the design of your investigation and how you obtained your sample, even though these are, strictly speaking, not usually included under the heading of 'procedure' in scientific reports.

Procedures followed in research practicals depend entirely on the nature of the project. There is no 'one size fits all' approach in conducting a study. We have already explored the steps taken in carrying out experiments and observations (Chapter 2). Studies using self-report are normally correlational or they are part of an experimental procedure. However, although details of procedures are method- and context-dependent, there are some basic common factors that can be identified. If you read any original report of an empirical study you should find that the method will be described according to the following standard steps, which include task procedure.

Nine steps in a practical investigation

(1) Decide aim/research question.

(2) Plan the investigation, including ensuring ethical guidelines will be followed, operationalising the hypothesis, preparing the materials/equipment.

(3) Recruit the sample (participants).

(4) Obtain informed consent from participants.

(5) Prepare for conduct of study.

(6) Follow task procedure (data collection).

(7) Debrief.

(8) Analyse data.

(9) Write report.

NB: The selection of nine steps is to help you remember the main stages – it is not prescriptive. That is to say that researchers do not consciously follow nine steps in conducting an investigation, but they will always pay attention to the checklist in Table 3.4 of things to do in order to ensure that they carry out their investigation effectively.

Table 3.4 Nine steps in conducting a practical investigation

	Experiment	Observation	Self-report
1	Decide aim, research question and alternate/null hypotheses	Decide aim and research question	Decide aim and research question
2	Plan procedure, including obtaining ethics approval, choosing experimental design, operationalising the hypothesis, preparation of materials and deciding sampling method	Plan procedure; obtain ethics approval, draw up schedule (if structured observation); choose and train observers; plan time and location for observation	Plan procedure; obtain ethics approval, decide sampling method; construct questionnaire or draw up interview questions
3	Obtain sample and make arrangement for conduct of study	Possibly run pilot study in order to check on usefulness of selected categories and feasibility	Organise distribution of self-report measure or organise interviews (if interview study)
4	Obtain informed consent from participants	Covert observation – no informed consent/overt observation – participants informed that observation will be conducted	Obtain informed consent from participants (usually done at same time as next step)
5	Allocate participants to experimental conditions and give instructions	Place observers in position	Distribute questionnaire
6	Participants follow experimental steps (data collected)	Conduct observation – participants are observed for designated period while observers record behaviours (data collected)	Participants respond to questionnaire (data collected)
7	Thank and debrief participants	Thank and debrief participants (overt observation)	Thank and debrief participants
8	Analyse data, produce findings and draw conclusions	Analyse data, produce findings and draw conclusions	Analyse data, produce findings and draw conclusions
9	Write report of practical investigation	Write report of practical investigation	Write report of practical investigation

3.6.1 Suggesting appropriate procedures in relation to source material

In the Psychological Investigations examination paper you will be given an outline of a research project and you may be asked to suggest an appropriate procedure in relation to the source material provided. You can be asked to outline a whole procedure or to focus on one aspect of procedure, such as sampling or measuring the dependent variable. The following three examples relate to an observation, an experiment and a study using a self-report questionnaire.

Observational procedure

Example 1 (Observation): Researchers want to conduct an observational study of students' use of laptops during their free time in college.

Q Describe and evaluate an appropriate procedure that could be used in this study. (10 marks)

A I would first decide to use a structured observation as this would allow quantitative data to be collected on student use of laptops. I would decide to use a covert observation as this would ensure that participants were unaware that they were being studied. This would lower the risk of demand characteristics and increase the ecological validity of the study.

I would then choose a time and location for running the observation. This study might be conducted for one hour over lunchtime and half an hour during morning and afternoon break every day for a week.

Two observers might be positioned in the student cafeteria during these times.

Time sampling might be used to record behaviours. Both observers might note down (tally) how many students were in the cafeteria and how many of them were using their laptops during every minute of the hour and half-hour break.

Observers' records might then be compared in order to measure inter-observer reliability.

The data could then be analysed and conclusions drawn about the amount of time students spend using their laptops in their free time. Mean laptop frequency could be calculated, and results for different days could be compared.

A strength of this procedure is that it should produce reliable data as the observation is structured and all behaviours are observed and recorded by two observers and their results compared. Another strength of the study is that it will be a valid study of student use of laptops in their free time as the covert nature ensures that the students are not aware that they are being studied and therefore would act normally. The covert nature of the observation can be seen as an ethical weakness, but as the observation takes place in a public area (a cafeteria) and does not involve sensitive behaviours, this is not a great weakness.

Here is another example for you to have a go at.

Example 2 (Observation): Researchers want to conduct an observation of children's play behaviours during morning and afternoon break at a primary school.

Q Describe and evaluate an appropriate procedure that could be used in this study. (10 marks)

Here are some hints as to what you should bear in mind when working out your procedure:

- What do you think your research question might be?
- Your answer will affect what type of observation you will conduct and your categories if you decide on a structured observation.
- If you decide on a structured observation, what sort of behaviours will you be noting down? Your answer might affect your decision as to whether to use time or event sampling.
- Event sampling is often more suitable for recording repeated short-term behaviours (e.g. running across the playground) whereas time sampling is usually more suited to behaviours that might last some time, such as sitting talking or playing football. Decide which one to use when you have determined which behaviours will be recorded.

When you have finished, see p.89 at the chapter end for an example of a suitable procedure.

Experimental procedure

Example 1 (Experiment): A researcher wants to conduct an experiment to investigate whether there is a difference in concentration levels of primary school pupils in the morning compared with the afternoon. Each pupil will be assessed in both the morning and the afternoon.

Q Describe and evaluate one way in which concentration could be measured in this investigation. (10 marks)

A In order to measure children's concentration I would choose a computer game in which participants were presented with two almost identical pictures in sequence that contained one difference. The children would have a choice of four words to choose from describing the difference. When they have chosen what the difference is, the computer gives them a mark if they are correct, then the next set of pictures appears in sequence. They will have ten sets of pictures to compare. This is a repeated measures design, so the computer program will have 20 sets of pictures altogether and each child will do ten sets in the morning and ten in the afternoon. The program will randomly generate ten of the pictures in random order during session 1 (morning) and then the other ten will be presented in random order during session 2 (afternoon). This will remove order effects. My sample will be a class of Year 6 primary school children whose parents have agreed to them taking part in the experiment. The dependent variable will be score correct out of ten in each session. Mean scores for the class during each session will be calculated to see whether there is a significant difference in scores between sessions. This will show whether there is a difference in pupil concentration levels in the morning and the afternoon.

A strength of the way concentration is measured in my study is that I have followed a controlled procedure that makes it possible to replicate my study. Another strength of the way in which concentration is measured is that because the picture pairs will be randomly generated for each child, this will to some extent remove order effects. However, a weakness of the procedure is that all the children were in the same class, so it was more practical to have them all do the experiment at the same time, which means that they all took the test for the first time in the morning and for the second time in the afternoon. This means that practice effects might be a confounding variable.

Another weakness of the way in which concentration is measured in this study is that although concentration is measured with spotting differences in pictures, the response the participants had to make involved reading words, which means that literacy could have affected the results. However, as the design of the study is repeated measures, literacy will not be a confounding variable as the children are competing against themselves. What it could mean, though, is that if some children could not read the words they might have made a low number of correct responses, which would mean that the test was not really a valid measure of concentration.

Here is another example for you to have a go at.

Example 2 (Experiment): A researcher has conducted an experiment to see whether secondary school-aged children's memory is affected by whether they learn and recall material in the same classroom compared with learning in one classroom and recalling in a different classroom. This was an independent measures design.

Q Describe and evaluate one way in which the effect of environment on children's recall ability could be measured in this investigation. (10 marks)

Hint – this question is focused on the way that recall is measured, not on the procedure of your study as a whole, so you should concentrate on the way in which you have measured recall and how reliable your measure is. A specimen answer will be found at the end of the chapter, p.90.

Self-report procedure

Example 1 (Self-report): A researcher has become interested in computer-related stress at work and wishes to conduct an investigation to assess stress levels in the workplace using the self-report method.

Q Describe and evaluate an appropriate sampling technique for this study. (10 marks)

A Computers are used in most workplaces nowadays. A study that aimed to investigate computer-related stress would need to be representative of a wide variety of workplaces and work roles. For this study I would identify several large employers in one city such as local government, a hospital, a university and several large firms. I would ask them to email around their employees and ask for volunteers to respond to an email questionnaire. Participants would be told that their responses would be seen by the researchers only and that no information would be passed to their employer.

The respondents would be asked to provide a contact number if they were willing to be interviewed and given a physiological assessment. The first few questions on the questionnaire would identify the number of hours the participant regularly spends working with computers in their job. Once the questionnaires had been collected in I would sample them to ensure that I had even numbers of respondents from each large employer working for set proportions of time with computers. I would sort responses according to the proportion of their working day spent working with computers (75%+, 50–74%, 25–49%, less than 25%). The data from all respondents would be analysed at the level of self-report responses regarding people's feelings about their work with computers and their experience of stress at work. I would then put all the respondents from each employer who worked for each set proportion of time into a hat and pull out names at random until 20 participants from each employer were selected who had offered to be available for further study. Those respondents would be approached and asked whether they would be willing to have a physiological stress measure taken at regular intervals during the day on three typical workdays.

This method of sampling is practical because it gives easy access to a very large number of workers in a variety of workplaces. However, it does not enable true random sampling as it is not possible to gain access to information on all employees, only to those willing to respond to the questionnaire. The stratified sampling method allows for selection of an even number of participants from each employer and each time bracket for physiological measures that could be used to assess reliability of the self-report responses with regard to experienced levels of stress.

Here is another example for you to have a go at.

Example 2 (Self-report): A researcher wants to conduct an investigation into student attitudes nationally towards A Level Psychology using the self-report method.

Q Describe and evaluate an appropriate sampling technique for this study. (10 marks)

Hint – If a study is aimed at investigating national attitudes it is important that your procedure enables a representative sample of the target population to be selected for participation. A specimen answer will be found at the end of the chapter, p.91.

Correlational procedure

Correlation is not a data-collecting method so it differs from the other methods in terms of discussion of procedure. You could only be asked to comment on data analysis with regard to correlation. If you were asked to discuss a procedure you would need to decide which data-collection method would be most suitable for providing your data. It is very likely to be self-report, although it could arguably involve observation. No examples are provided because for procedure you would in these cases refer back to self-report procedure.

3.6.2 Longitudinal versus snapshot methods

One more important issue in terms of study procedure that you should be aware of is whether an investigation has been conducted over a period of time (longitudinal) or on one occasion (snapshot/cross-sectional). This does not refer to how long the experimenters took to collect their data, but rather to the length of time of each participant's involvement and also the aim of the study. If you take **Baron-Cohen's** study, for example, each individual with autism or Tourette's syndrome was individually tested in a suitable environment. This research may have taken Baron-Cohen several weeks or months to complete, but it is nevertheless described as 'snapshot' because each participant did the test on only one occasion, hence we see a 'snapshot' of their theory of mind ability. **Baron-Cohen** could have made this longitudinal research. In this case his aim would have been to find out whether people with autism have stable abilities in this task or whether they continue to develop better abilities with age. If he had decided to take a longitudinal approach he would have had to prepare several different sets of photos and used a different one each time he tested the individual (say, once a year for five years).

> **Extend Your Understanding**
>
> **Fuzzy areas**
>
> There are, of course, some studies that are hard to classify. This is because things in real life are fuzzier than psychologists would sometimes like them to be. Studies described as snapshot can last a relatively long time if a) the study has a repeated-measures design, or b) the nature of the study means that it is of relatively long duration. How does one classify a study that lasts several days, for example? Probably the best approach to take is to focus on the aim of the experiment. It is normally classed as longitudinal only if the main aim of the investigation is to explore the effect of one or more variables over time.

Strengths of longitudinal/snapshot procedures

● A strength of snapshot research is that it is relatively easy to organise and provides immediate results.

● A strength of longitudinal research is that it provides rich data about participants, enabling us to understand development (change over time) and it can also enable predictions about effects of variables to be made. You will find more on this in the A2 section of this book, p.156–7.

Table 3.5 Longitudinal versus snapshot methods in the Core Studies

Study	Longitudinal or snapshot?	Evidence
Loftus and Palmer	Snapshot	Participants sat the memory experiment on one occasion – true, in the second experiment they came back a week later and asked about broken glass, but this was an integral part of the same snapshot.
Baron-Cohen *et al.*	Snapshot	Participants took the Reading the Mind in the Eyes test on one occasion.
Savage-Rumbaugh	**Longitudinal**	Kanzi's language development was studied intensively over a period of 18 months.
Samuel and Bryant	Snapshot	Children of different ages were tested on one occasion for conservation ability.
Bandura *et al.*	Snapshot	Children were studied on one occasion for imitation of aggressive behaviour.
Freud	**Longitudinal**	Little Hans's behaviour was studied by his father and reported to Freud over a period of years.
Dement and Kleitman	Snapshot	Although some participants participated several times (sleeping in a laboratory on several nights), this was a variant on repeated measures as the experimenter adopted different waking schedules.
Sperry	Snapshot	Patients who had undergone deconnective surgery were tested on one occasion to take a snapshot of the effects of the surgery on their perceptual functioning.
Maguire *et al.*	Snapshot	Taxi drivers were put once in the MRI scanner and their data compared with scans of non-taxi drivers who had also been scanned once.
Piliavin *et al.*	Snapshot	This one may look deceptive as it was conducted over a period of months, but the data were all analysed together – the time period was to enable a big sample size to be studied, not to investigate change over time.
Milgram	Snapshot	Participants were put through Milgram's obedience experiment on only one occasion.
Reicher and Haslam	Longitudinal	This is a slightly fuzzy one. Participants stayed in the simulated prison environment for ten days and changes in their behaviour were observed over this period, but in terms of longitudinal research this is of short duration.
Rosenhan	Snapshot/longitudinal	This is another fuzzy one. This could have been just a 'snapshot' because the key point of the study was whether the pseudopatients would be admitted to hospital or not – if the authorities had seen through the deception, the study would have ended immediately. However, some of the pseudopatients ended up staying a long time (several weeks) and they conducted observations over that time.
Thigpen and Cleckley	Longitudinal	Thigpen and Cleckley's patient with multiple personality disorder attended therapy sessions over a period of time and during this time other personalities emerged.
Griffiths	Snapshot	Participants took part in the gambling experiment on one occasion.

3.7 Data analysis

Data collection is undertaken through experiments, observational studies and self-report measures, e.g. questionnaires. Data can be qualitative or quantitative.

3.7.1 Qualitative and quantitative data

(a) Qualitative data

Qualitative data are data that are not numerical. They are descriptive data. They can be a rich source of information on behaviours and attitudes. In order to draw meaningful conclusions from qualitative data it is usually necessary to impose structure on the raw data. For example, content analysis can be used to analyse texts or interviews for common themes.

- A strength of qualitative data is that they are not limited by preselected categories and therefore enable full description of behaviour, feelings or attitudes.

- A weakness of qualitative data is that they can be difficult to analyse and make comparisons or to draw meaningful conclusions from.

(b) Quantitative data

Most psychological investigations today collect quantitative data. Quantitative data are numerical data (e.g. scores on tests) that can be analysed statistically in order to provide comparisons between groups of participants or to show statistically meaningful relationships between variables. One of the reasons that quantitative data are commonly collected today is that sophisticated computer programs (e.g. SPSS) enable vast quantities of numerical data to be analysed according to a variety of methods. Even though programs such as SPSS facilitate data analysis, it is still important to understand the statistical principles that such computer programs employ. In particular it should be noted that the results are reliable only if the data collection and inputting are done correctly and the appropriate statistical test is applied. At AS Level you need to understand only the basics of descriptive statistics, but at A2 Level you will also need to understand a few basic inferential-statistics tests (see p.107–9).

- A strength of quantitative data is that they allow statistical analysis, enabling cause and effect to be measured and relationships between variables to be analysed

- A weakness of quantitative data is that they can impose limited choices on participants and by imposing categories can miss out on potentially important aspects of behaviour or feelings.

NB: Although most modern studies collect quantitative data, it is possible in one study to collect *both* qualitative and quantitative data, as you will see from Table 3.6.

3.7.2 Qualitative and quantitative data in the Core Studies

Examine Table 3.6 and you will see how many of the Core Studies collected quantitative data and how many collected qualitative data. Can you see any patterns in terms of approaches or dates of publication and type of data collected?

Table 3.6 Qualitative and quantitative data in the Core Studies

Study	Date of study	Data type	Data summary
Loftus and Palmer	1974	Quantitative	Estimated recalled speed
Baron-Cohen et al.	1997	Quantitative	Score on Reading the Mind in the Eyes task
Savage-Rumbaugh	1986	Quantitative and **qualitative**	Number of lexigrams used and understood (quantitative measure) but also descriptive data of Kanzi's behaviour
Samuel and Bryant	1984	Quantitative	Number of errors on conservation task
Bandura et al.	1961	Quantitative	Number of imitative and non-imitative aggressive behaviours observed
Freud	1909	**Qualitative**	Father's observations of Little Hans's behaviour and report of Hans's feelings and dreams
Dement and Kleitman	1957	Quantitative and **qualitative**	Quantitative – EEG record of electrical activity and eye movements; number of dreams recalled after REM and NREM sleep. Qualitative – dream content
Sperry	1968	**Qualitative**	Description of impairment in perceptual tasks shown in patients who had undergone surgery for epilepsy
Maguire et al.	2000	Quantitative	MRI scans analysed for grey matter volume and density
Piliavin et al.	1969	Quantitative and **qualitative**	Quantitative- latency before help was given to a 'victim' Qualitative – recorded observations of participants' reactions and comments about the 'victim'
Milgram	1963	Quantitative and **qualitative**	Quantitative – voltage to which participants were prepared to go to in administering 'shocks' Qualitative – recorded observations of participants' reactions to the experiment, e.g. signs of stress; hysterical laughter
Reicher and Haslam	2006	**Qualitative**	Observed behavioural consequences of prison simulation and planned interventions
Rosenhan	1973	**Qualitative**	Observed reactions of hospital staff to pseudopatients' self-referral and subsequent interactions between pseudopatients and staff
Thigpen and Cleckley	1954	**Qualitative**	Clinical observations of behaviour of a patient who presented with symptoms of multiple personality disorder
Griffiths	1994	Quantitative and **qualitative**	Quantitative – observed number of plays, number of wins, amount won Qualitative – recorded verbal protocols (self-report of feelings during play)

From this point on this section will deal essentially with issues relating to quantitative data analysis.

3.7.3 Descriptive statistics

Once quantitative data have been collected, descriptive statistics are used to present, summarise and describe the findings. Descriptive statistics are statistics that simply describe the data rather than subjecting the data to tests of statistical significance. At AS Level it is sufficient to under-stand the basic elements of descriptive statistics.

You need to know about:

- measures of central tendency (averages): mode, median and mean
- measures of dispersion, for example the range of the data
- graphical representations of data, for example bar charts.

The first stage of dealing with data is to 'eyeball' it. This means to look carefully at the raw data to spot some obvious characteristics.

Let's have a look at a set of data from one of the Core Studies. Baron-Cohen in his study on advanced theory of mind reported the mean score and range of scores of each group of participants but not individual participants' scores so we are going to work with some imaginary data based on his reported means and ranges for each group.

Table 3.7 Imagined scores of participants with Austism (n = 16) and participants with Tourette's Syndrome (n=10) on Baron-Cohen's Reading the Mind in the Eyes Task

Autism group	Score of correct responses out of 25	TS group	Score of correct responses out of 25
1	17	1	22
2	16	2	20
3	14	3	17
4	14	4	16
5	21	5	25
6	13	6	22
7	15	7	19
8	18	8	22
9	23	9	23
10	18	10	18
11	15		
12	15		
13	16		
14	14		
15	16		
16	16		

Just by looking at the data and not performing any calculations you can see that the scores of the participants in the Tourette's group look higher than those with autism. However, if you want to make more meaningful comparisons between the two groups you will need to perform a basic statistical operation. You will need to know how to calculate a measure of central tendency and a measure of the dispersion of the data.

3.7.4 Measures of central tendency

A measure of central tendency refers to one numerical value that best represents the data (an average). This can be the mean, median or mode. In order to gain a fuller understanding of the spread of your data, a measure of dispersion (e.g. range) is also frequently calculated.

(a) Mean

The mean is calculated by adding together all the values in the dataset and dividing by the number of values. Do this calculation for the data above. You will need to sum (add up) the individual scores in each group and then divide them by the number of scores in that group. Your calculation should look like this:

Scores of participants with autism:

$13+14+14+14+15+15+15+16+16+16+16+17+18+18+21+23 = 261$
$261 \div 16 = 16.3$

Mean score of participants with autism = 16.3, range 13–23.

Scores of participants with tourettes:

$16+17+18+19+20+22+22+22+23+25 = 204$
$204 \div 10 = 20.4$

By comparing the mean scores we can see that the results appear to support the eyeballed conclusion that participants with autism performed less well on the task than participants with tourettes. The mean gives an arithmetically accurate average score for each group, which we can compare to see if the alternate hypothesis was supported or not. For measuring things such as time, or weight or height or anything where decimal accuracy has real meaning, the mean average is usually the best and most accurate measure of central tendency to work with. However, there is a problem with the mean here, as it can give us what is called 'spurious accuracy'. The means for the participants in each group were as follows: participants with autism, mean = 16.3; participants with tourettes, mean = 20.4. Neither of these means represents even one true score in the set of scores that they represent.

For this reason it is sometimes better to use an alternative measure of central tendency, the median or the mode.

(b) Median

There are two circumstances in which the median can be a more useful measure of central tendency than the mean. The first is when you are measuring whole numbers such as scores on a rating scale. The other is when you have a combination of a relatively small set of scores and one score that is very high or low and therefore distorts or skews the mean. The median identifies the central point of a set of scores. The median is worked out by putting all the scores in size order (this is done for you in the calculation above) and finding the central point. If there is an even number of scores in the set you take a mean of the middle two scores to find the median.

To find the median for the autism group you find the central two scores (since there is an even number of scores), add them and divide by two. The eighth and ninth scores are both 16. The mean of these two scores is therefore also 16. The median for this set is 16. Now we have a whole number to represent a set made of whole numbers, and it even represents four of the actual scores. In this instance it could be argued that the median is a better (more representative) average than the mean. The fifth and sixth scores of the participants with tourettes are 20 and 22 respectively. The median of the tourettes participants is therefore 21. Again we now have a whole number, but one that does not represent any actual score from the set. In reporting his actual findings, Baron–Cohen cited the mean but he might alternatively have cited the median as in this case it might have been a better (more representative) measure of central tendency than the mean. As Baron–Cohen did not report his raw data, though, we are not in a position to judge this.

(c) Mode

There are instances, however, when the median is not particularly representative of the data we are analysing. If you have a small set of scores and one score clearly predominates, it may be better to calculate the mode. This simply tells us the most frequently occurring value in the set. For example, in the case of our imagined data the mode for the group of participants with autism is 16 and the mode for the group of participants with tourettes is 22. The mode will always represent at least two scores in the actual set of scores, but loses its meaningfulness if there are more than two modes. Of course, if each score occurs only once in a set then there is no mode, so this measure of central tendency is not useful where all items are different in the set. On this occasion the median and mode happen to be the same for the group with autism but not for the tourettes group.

3.7.5 Calculating measures of central tendency and suggesting appropriate measures of central tendency in relation to source material

In the G541: Psychological Investigations exam you may be presented with sample data and asked to calculate one measure of central tendency and then comment on whether it is the most suitable measure of central tendency for analysing the data provided. Here is an example.

Researchers wanted to conduct an experiment to investigate the ability of seven children aged 6 and eight children aged 9 to identify basic emotions in faces. The participants were shown two sets of six photographs of the same person displaying in each case a different basic emotion (sadness, happiness, surprise, anger, disgust, fear). The experimenter then asked the following question each time: 'What do you think the person in the photograph is feeling?' One mark was recorded for each correct response, giving a maximum possible score on each set of six.

Table 3.8 Raw data from basic emotions task

	Six-year-old children Score out of 6 Set 1	Six-year-old children Score out of 6 Set 2	Nine-year-old children Score out of 6 Set 1	Nine-year-old children Score out of 6 Set 2
P1	4	4	6	6
P2	2	3	6	5
P3	2	2	4	5
P4	3	3	5	5
P5	1	2	6	6
P6	2	2	5	6
P7	4	4	3	3
P8			6	6

Q 1. Explain what is meant by the descriptive statistic the mean. (2 marks)

A The mean is a measure of central tendency that is calculated by adding the values (e.g. scores) in a set and dividing by the number of values (scores) to find the numerical average.

Q 2. Explain how the mean would have been calculated for the six year olds and nine year olds in this study. (4 marks)

A First you would find total score per participant over the two sets. Then you would add up the total scores for each candidate in the six-year-old group and divide by 7 (the number of participants). You would then do the same for the nine-year-old group but divide by 8. This would give you mean scores (out of 12) for both groups. The mean for the six year olds is 5.71 and for the nine year olds is 10.37.

Q 3. When would the descriptive statistic called the 'median' be more appropriate and why? (4 marks)

A The descriptive statistic called the median might be more appropriate for a study such as that outlined above. This is because you are dealing with whole numbers. This can give you a mean that is not a whole number and is not representative of any of the scores actually achieved by any of the children. If you calculate the median (middle) score for each group it will be a whole number and probably representative of scores achieved by several participants. This will be more representative of the data. In this case the median score for the six year olds is 5 and the median for the nine year olds is 11. These scores are more representative of the scores obtained by the participants than the mean scores.

Here is another example for you to try. You will find a likely answer given on p.92.

A researcher wanted to conduct an experiment to investigate whether there is a difference in the concentration of secondary school students in the morning compared with the afternoon. Ten students were assessed using two pairs of spot-the-difference puzzles that had ten differences in each pair. One pair of puzzles was given to the children in the morning and one in the afternoon. Each time the children were given five minutes to spot as many differences as possible. This was a repeated measures design.

Table 3.9 Raw data from concentration task

	Number of differences spotted Condition 1 (morning)	Number of differences spotted Condition 2 (afternoon)
P1	9	9
P2	7	8
P3	7	6
P4	9	7
P5	10	9
P6	9	8
P7	6	7
P8	9	10
P9	7	6
P10	9	7

Q 1. Explain what is meant by the descriptive statistic the median. (2 marks)

Q 2. Explain how the mean would have been calculated for participants in each condition.(2 marks)

Q 3. When would the descriptive statistic called the 'mode' be more appropriate and why? (4 marks)

3.7.6 Measures of dispersion – the range

As well as being able to summarise a set of scores by looking at central, average or typical scores, it is useful to know how widely dispersed or spread out the scores are. To calculate the range of a set of scores you simply subtract the lowest score in the set from the highest score. In the example above (Table 3.9), the lowest score in both conditions is 6 and the highest score in both conditions is 10, so the range (calculated by subtracting 6 from 10) in both cases is 4. This tells us that the range is similar in both conditions even though the average (however calculated) shows a difference between conditions. In the earlier example (Table 3.8), however, the range of scores of the six-year-old children was 5 (8 − 3) while the range for older children was 6 (12 − 6). This shows a slightly wider variation in basic-emotion recognition in older children than younger ones.

3.7.7 Graphical representations of data

(a) Bar charts

Bar charts are a useful and meaningful way of presenting summarised data from an experiment. Bar charts should not show scores of individual participants but should be drawn based on a measure of central tendency for each condition (normally the mean) and bars should be drawn to show calculated difference between the two conditions.

For example, Figure 3.1 is a bar chart showing mean scores calculated from the raw data in Table 3.8.

Q Now draw a bar chart representing the data in Table 3.9.

See the end of the chapter, p.93, for a specimen example.

You might also be asked to draw conclusions from data presented in a bar graph. As long as you read carefully the axis labels, the title and any key, this should be straightforward.

Q Having drawn your graph, what conclusions can you draw about the difference in group performance shown?

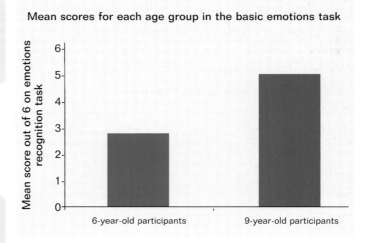

Figure 3.1

(b) Correlations

You might also be asked to draw a scattergraph in response to correlational data, or to interpret data presented in scattergraph format. See Chapter 2, p.40, for examples.

Answers

3.1.2 Informed consent

Table 3.10 Informed consent reported in the Core Studies

Study	Date	Approach	Informed consent reported
Loftus and Palmer	1974	Cognitive	**No**
Baron-Cohen et al.	1997	Cognitive	Yes
Savage-Rumbaugh	1986	Cognitive	**No – impossible with animal participants**
Samuel and Bryant	1984	Developmental	**No – no report of parental consent obtained**
Bandura et al.	1961	Developmental	**No – no report of parental consent obtained**
Freud	1909	Developmental	Yes – parental request
Dement and Kleitman	1957	Physiological	Yes
Sperry	1968	Physiological	Yes
Maguire et al.	2000	Physiological	Yes
Piliavin et al.	1969	Social	**No – impossible in covert field experiment**
Milgram	1963	Social	Yes
Reicher and Haslam	2006	Social	Yes
Rosenhan	1973	Individual differences	**No – covert study**
Thigpen and Cleckley	1954	Individual differences	Yes – patient self-referral
Griffiths	1994	Individual differences	Yes

3.1.3 Deception
Table 3.11 Deception in the Core Studies

Study	Date	Approach	Deception practised
Loftus and Palmer	1974	Cognitive	No
Baron-Cohen et al.	1997	Cognitive	No
Savage-Rumbaugh	1986	Cognitive	No
Samuel and Bryant	1984	Developmental	No
Bandura et al.	1961	Developmental	Yes – children were exposed to simulated aggression, which was deceptive
Freud	1909	Developmental	No
Dement and Kleitman	1957	Physiological	Yes, in one case the participant was deceived with regard to his waking schedule
Sperry	1968	Physiological	No
Maguire et al.	2000	Physiological	No
Piliavin et al.	1969	Social	Yes – passengers deceived into thinking a fellow passenger had collapsed
Milgram	1963	Social	Yes – participants were deceived into believing they were administering potentially lethal electric shocks to fellow participants
Reicher and Haslam	2006	Social	No
Rosenhan	1973	Individual differences	Yes – hospital staff were deceived into admitting healthy people pretending to have a psychological disorder (Study 1) and into believing in a follow-up study that pseudopatients would try for admission
Thigpen and Cleckley	1954	Individual differences	No
Griffiths	1994	Individual differences	No

3.1.4 Right to withdraw
Table 3.12 Right to withdraw in the Core Studies

Study	Date	Approach	Right to withdraw reported	Right to withdraw possible in practice
Loftus and Palmer	1974	Cognitive	No	Yes
Baron-Cohen et al.	1997	Cognitive	No	Yes
Savage-Rumbaugh	1986	Cognitive	No	No – impossible for captive animals to withdraw
Samuel and Bryant	1984	Developmental	No	No – difficult for a child in a school setting to refuse
Bandura et al.	1961	Developmental	No	No – even though some children were upset they were made to continue
Freud	1909	Developmental	No	No – impossible for Little Hans to withdraw as his father was collecting the data
Dement and Kleitman	1957	Physiological	No	Yes, some participants reported only once or twice for sleep in the laboratory and then withdrew
Sperry	1968	Physiological	Yes	Yes
Maguire et al.	2000	Physiological	Yes	Yes
Piliavin et al.	1969	Social	No	No – impossible as the passengers were not aware of the fact they were participating in a study
Milgram	1963	Social	Yes –all participants were informed of their right to withdraw	Yes, some participants withdrew but were strongly discouraged by the responses of the confederate who told them that they had to go on
Reicher and Haslam	2006	Social	No	Yes, but it would have been difficult for participants to withdraw once filming started
Rosenhan	1973	Individual differences	No	No – impossible in Study 1 as the participants (hospital staff) were not aware they were participating in a study
Thigpen and Cleckley	1954	Individual differences	Yes	Yes, in fact the participant did eventually withdraw from treatment by the researchers
Griffiths	1994	Individual differences	Yes	Yes

3.1.5 Debrief
Table 3.13 Debrief reported in the Core Studies

Study	Date	Approach	Debrief reported
Loftus and Palmer	1974	Cognitive	**No**
Baron-Cohen et al.	1997	Cognitive	**No**
Savage-Rumbaugh	1986	Cognitive	**No – impossible to debrief animals**
Samuel and Bryant	1984	Developmental	**No**
Bandura et al.	1961	Developmental	**No**
Freud	1909	Developmental	**No**
Dement and Kleitman	1957	Physiological	**No**
Sperry	1968	Physiological	**No**
Maguire et al.	2000	Physiological	**No**
Piliavin et al.	1969	Social	**No – impossible as study was an ongoing covert observation**
Milgram	1963	Social	Yes, participants were fully debriefed afterwards, including being informed as to the deception that had been practised on them
Reicher and Haslam	2006	Social	Yes
Rosenhan	1973	Individual differences	**No**
Thigpen and Cleckley	1954	Individual differences	Yes, as the therapy sessions were a form of debrief
Griffiths	1994	Individual differences	Yes, and regular gamblers were offered help with their addiction as part of the debrief

3.1.6 Confidentiality/anonymity
Studies that broke anonymity were both case studies – Savage-Rumbaugh and Freud. Animals are not seen as having a right to anonymity and primates such as Kanzi become famous. Freud named the parents of Little Hans, thus allowing him to be identified. In Thigpen and Cleckley the patient was given a pseudonym but later chose to reveal her identity.

3.1.7 Responses to ethics issues in source material

(b) Ways of dealing with ethical issues
A1. One ethical issue was that this study was a covert observation. This means that participants were not aware that they were being observed and informed consent was not obtained.

A second ethical issue was that as this study was an ongoing covert observation lasting all day, the participants could not be debriefed immediately as it would have affected their behaviour at other times during the day and they might have told other students what was happening, which would have affected the results.

A2. Students might have been informed that an observation was going to be conducted one day that week on campus and that they would be invited afterwards to a debrief session.

3.2.1 Reliability and validity in the Core Studies

A1. The effect of asking one or two questions in testing children's ability to conserve was reliably measured in Samuel and Bryant's experiment because the procedure was completely standardised and the experimenter always used the same wording in asking the questions.

NB: You could, however, answer that you do not think this a very reliable measure because the children might think that they have to answer a certain way to please the experimenter.

A2. The experiment appears to have good face validity because it appears to test children's understanding of conservation using the same materials Piaget used in his original study and the only thing that is different in the two conditions is the experimenter-manipulated IV (one or two questions).

A3. As noted above, the study has face validity and is high in ecological validity as it tests real children in their own school environment. Also, the measure appears to be reliable because the way it is operationalised is standardised. We can therefore conclude that Samuel and Bryant's study is a valid study of the effects of asking one or two questions in Piaget's conservation task.

3.2.2 Responses to questions of reliability/validity in the source material

Reliability means consistency of the measure whereas validity in this context means whether the measure actually measures what the researchers want it to. In this study the procedure was standardised in that the participants were given a list of ten words to look at for one minute each time and each time they were asked to recall as many words as they could immediately afterwards. This standardisation should contribute towards reliability of the measure. However, the source material does not provide information about how similar the lists of words were. If one list contained harder or less familiar words then the measure will not be consistent (reliable). This could have been controlled for by giving half of the children one list (list A) while listening to music and the other half list B while listening to music, and then swapping round. This would have ensured greater reliability of the measure.

The validity of the measure is affected by the fact that, as has been shown, the measure was not particularly reliable. Also the validity is affected by the fact that the study is supposed to be about concentration but in fact it probably measures other things such as literacy and memory skills rather than concentration. This means that the experiment has low face validity. The study is quite high in ecological validity, however, as it is like the kind of learning task that children have to do at school or at home and it is quite realistic that children might try to learn for a test while playing music or in silence. Validity would have been improved if the study had tested concentration without testing memory. For example, children could have been tested by spotting mistakes in a list of words rather than having to remember a list afterwards. However, the study would still not have been valid unless the reliability was improved by making sure that the two sets of stimulus materials were closely matched or unless half the children had one set (set A) while listening to music and the other had the other set (set B) while listening to music. You could control for other aspects of order effects by making sure that half the children did the task with music first while the other half did it in silence first. This would have improved the validity of the study.

3.2.3 Ecological validity in the Core Studies

Table 3.1 Answers Ecological validity in the Core Studies

NB: These are likely responses but you may have different views – this is acceptable as long as you can cite evidence in support of your answer.

Study	High/Low in ecological validity	Evidence
Loftus and Palmer	Low	Video clips, not real-life accident.
Baron-Cohen et al.	Low	Still photos of faces, not moving.
Savage-Rumbaugh	Mixed	Low in ecological validity as bonobos were in captivity, but high in ecological validity in terms of investigating the role of environment in language acquisition.
Samuel and Bryant	High	Real children in a classroom environment doing a learning task.
Bandura et al.	Mixed	Real children in a nursery environment but ecological validity marred by the fact that the adults in the nursery were known and trusted by the children and did not usually act in an aggressive manner.
Freud	High	Real-life interactions of a little boy with his parents.
Dement and Kleitman	Low	People do not sleep in a lab with electrodes on their heads.
Sperry	Mixed	In normal life people who have undergone hemisphere deconnection can gain information through all their senses and do not display the problems highlighted under the controlled conditions of the study.
Maguire et al.	N/A	Ecological validity is not relevant in a study that involved only structural brain scans.
Piliavin et al.	High	Real-life situation on subway with real passengers. The victim, however, pretended to be ill but it must have been realistic as people almost always tried to help.

Table 3.1 Answers continued

Study	High/Low in ecological validity	Evidence
Milgram	Mixed	Although this study took place in a lab with an experimenter present (apparently low in ecological validity), the study wanted to test obedience in this sort of environment so was actually quite realistic – and quite similar to what some people were ordered to do during the Second World War.
Reicher and Haslam	Mixed	The experimenters took pains to try to make the situation (simulated prison) as close to real life as possible, but the participants were always aware that it was just a simulation.
Rosenhan	High	The experimenters took on the role of patients in real hospitals for people with psychological disorders.
Thigpen and Cleckley	Mixed	The therapy situation was real-life but the researchers did not visit the patient in her own home so they did not observe her behaviour in a normal environment.
Griffiths	Mixed	This was realistic in that it took place in a real gambling arcade but ecological validity was reduced by the fact that the participants were not gambling with their own money.

3.2.3 Ecological validity in source material
Ecological validity can be defined as how like real life an investigation is. This experiment has both strengths and weaknesses in terms of ecological validity. It is high in ecological validity because it tests actual students in a real-life situation of revising for exams. Students often revise while listening to music on an i-Pod and some students will choose to revise in a quiet atmosphere, so both conditions are ecologically valid. However, the ecological validity of the investigation is negatively affected by the fact that the students all revise in the same room, listening to the same loud music, while the students in the quiet condition are all placed in a silent classroom. These conditions are quite different from real life. Students who listen to music while revising will probably have their own i-Pod and listen to music that they like at a noise level they are comfortable with. The silent room is also not that ecologically valid as although people were asked to keep quiet, they were all together in one classroom whereas students probably revise on their own or in a small group in real life and they would not have to stay completely silent even if they were revising in quiet conditions.

3.3.2 Hypotheses in source material
An appropriate null hypothesis is that no significant relationship will be found between female college students' self-rating of importance of physical appearance and reported amount of exercise taken per week.

3.4.2 Identifying and operationalising/measuring the IV and DV in source material
A1. The independent variable was whether the children had been trained or not.

A2. The independent variable was whether children had been trained in identifying emotions in faces or not. The trained group had been read a story and shown faces expressing the basic emotions discussed in the story on the day before the experiment was conducted. The control group had not been trained.

A3. The dependent variable was score on a basic emotion identification task.

A4. The dependent variable was measured by each child being shown six photographs of the same person displaying the six basic emotions (sadness, happiness, surprise, anger, disgust, fear) and then responding to a question asked by the experimenter about how the person in the photograph was feeling. The number of correct responses made by each child was recorded. The result of the study was determined by adding up the scores of the children in each group, dividing the total group score by the number of participants in each group and then comparing group mean scores on the task.

3.5.2 Sampling in the Core Studies

Table 3.3 Answers Sampling method in the Core Studies

Core Study	Sampling clearly identified (circle yes or no)	If stated, which method was used?	If not stated, which method do you think was used? Probable answers – supporting evidence varies Bold = almost without doubt Italics = probably
Loftus and Palmer	No		*Opportunity (could be self-selected but unlikely due to high numbers)*
Baron-Cohen *et al.*	Yes	Self-selected/ opportunity: Baron-Cohen stated that one group were volunteers from the local population (the control group) but he does not state how he obtained the clinical samples – probably through a hospital register, which makes those groups opportunity samples.	
Savage-Rumbaugh	No		**Opportunity (animals can't volunteer)**
Samuel and Bryant	No		*Opportunity (could be self-selected but unlikely as participants were young children and schools involved in research usually operate a right-to-withdraw policy – that is, they ask for permission from parents for a child to participate in any research project being conducted and parents need to write in if they do not want their child to participate)*

Table 3.3 Answers continued

Core Study	Sampling clearly identified (circle yes or no)	If stated, which method was used?	If not stated, which method do you think was used? *Probable answers – supporting evidence varies* **Bold = almost without doubt** *Italics = probably*
Bandura *et al.*	No		*Opportunity (for same as reason stated above)*
Freud	No		*Opportunity/self-selected: child 'volunteered' by father*
Dement and Kleitman	No		**Self-selected: this is not stated but the nature of this study makes an opportunity sample impossible. Can you imagine standing outside a lab and asking anyone who came along if they would like to sleep there that night with electrodes on their heads?**
Sperry	No		*Opportunity/volunteer: probably all patients who had undergone this operation were directly contacted and asked to participate, which makes it opportunity rather than volunteer*
Maguire *et al.*	No		*Self-selected: the taxi drivers were probably volunteers, as were probably the normal controls whose data were used for comparison*
Piliavin *et al.*	Yes	Opportunity (covert): passengers on the New York subway	
Milgram	Yes	Self-selected: Milgram advertised for paid volunteers from the local community	
Reicher and Haslam	Yes	Self-selected (and then selection process): Reicher and Haslam advertised for participants in their televised study and then screened over 300 applicants, who were whittled down to 15 by the experimenters	
Rosenhan	No	Not stated but clearly opportunity as this was a covert study	
Thigpen and Cleckley	No		*Opportunity – although the patient volunteered for treatment, once she became Thigpen and Cleckley's patient she became an opportunity sample for their research*
Griffiths	Yes	Self-selected/opportunity: Griffiths advertised for non-gamblers (controls) but he approached gamblers and asked them to participate	

3.5.3 Suggest/outline appropriate samples/sampling methods in source material

In answering this question you could suggest any of the three main sampling methods so long as you can justify your answer. For example:

An appropriate sampling method that could be used would be random sampling. This would entail getting a computer to generate 100 names randomly from a database containing the names of all the female students at one college. I would choose this method because every student would have an equal chance of being picked and this should ensure that the sample is representative of the target population (female college students) and there would be no obvious biases in the selection process.

or

An appropriate sampling method that could be used for this study would be a self-selected sample. I would distribute posters and leaflets around a college advertising my study and would ask female students to volunteer by sending me an email so that I could email them my questionnaire for them to fill in.

or

An appropriate sampling method that could be used for this study would be an opportunity sample. I would stand in a busy area of the campus, such as outside the student cafeteria, and ask all the female students who passed by if they minded spending a few minutes answering the questions in my questionnaire. I would collect in the questionnaires when they had finished.

3.5.4 Identify strengths and weaknesses of sampling techniques described in source material

Strength: Likely answers will indicate that a strength of the sampling method is that it meets a high level of ethical standards as both schools and parents were self-selecting. An alternative strength is that it is an easy and practical way of obtaining a sample that is from the target population.

Weakness: Likely answers will indicate that the sample may be unrepresentative or biased. Good answers may point out that the number obtained is small in comparison with the possible target numbers (four schools with two classes of 30 each makes a possible maximum sample of 240 students but only 30 were volunteered by parents). Alternatively, strong answers may indicate that a likely source of bias is that the schools/parents that are willing for their children to participate in literacy research will probably produce a sample biased towards high literacy.

3.6.1 Suggesting appropriate procedures in relation to source material

Observational procedure

Example 2 (Observation): I would decide in advance what categories of behaviours I was interested in recording. I would then decide how often to conduct an observation. For example, I might run the observation every morning and afternoon break for a week. I would station observers where they could see all parts of the playground, two to each area. The observers would be teachers in the school so that the children were not made anxious by the presence of strangers.

I might choose to record particular behaviours such as playing ball, running around, talking to a friend, and I would record each time I saw a child engaged in these activities. I would also record whether the child was a boy or a girl. Event sampling might be used to record frequency of these behaviours. Both observers in each area of the playground would keep a tally of how many times during each break boys and girls engaged in these activities. Observers' records might then be compared in order to measure inter-observer reliability.

The data could then be analysed and conclusions drawn about the frequency of different behaviours and whether there were gendered patterns of behaviour shown. Mean frequency for boys and girls could be calculated for each behaviour and the results compared.

A strength of this procedure is that it should produce reliable data as the observation is structured and all observers would observe the same behaviours. Another strength of the procedure outlined is that two observers are placed in each area of the playground so their results can be checked for reliability. Another strength of the study is that it will be a valid study of playground behaviours because the children are used to their teachers being in the playground and will not realise that they are being observed and will behave normally. The covert nature of the observation can be seen as an ethical weakness, but as the observation is conducted by the children's teachers in the normal life of the school day, this is this is not a great weakness. Another weakness of the procedure is that only certain pre-agreed behaviours are tallied and the categories may not cover all observed behaviours. Another weakness of the study is that there would probably be a great many children in each area of the playground and they will be moving around a lot, so it may be difficult for observers to record behaviours accurately. Sometimes observers in different areas may tally the same child by mistake.

You would not need to make all these points to gain full marks – and you could make other, equally valid points to gain marks. Try to assess whether you have enough to gain ten marks.

Experimental procedure
Example 2 (Experiment): First I would prepare my materials. I would choose a list of ten difficult words. Then I would select my sample. I would use a random-sampling method for choosing my participants. I would ask the school to put the names of all the pupils in the school into a database and randomly select 40 names. I would then randomly allocate 20 of the children to condition A (same classroom) and 20 to condition B (different classroom). In condition A I would give the 20 children one minute to study the list of words. Then I would take the list away. I would give them a short distractor task in the same classroom (talking to their neighbour for one minute without discussing the word list). Then I would give the participants a pen and paper and ask them to recall as many words as possible from the list.

In condition B I would give the children the same list of words to learn in the same amount of time. However once they had finished I would get them to move to a different classroom. I would let them talk to each other while they moved but I would tell them not to discuss the word list. Once they were seated in another classroom I would hand out pens and paper and ask them to recall as many words as possible from the list. I would calculate mean scores of correctly recalled words for each group and compare the results between the two conditions.

A strength of the way I have measured the effect of environment is that I randomly selected participants and randomly allocated them to groups, which should control participant variables. A weakness of this method, though, is that because I have got only 20 participants in each condition and the school probably has hundreds of pupils, I may have ended up with two groups of different mean ages or abilities. It may have been better to use a matched pairs design instead of independent samples in this investigation. A strength of the way in which I measured the dependent variable was that I controlled the procedure well –all the children had the same list of words and the same time to learn them in, and children in both conditions were allowed to talk between learning and recall. However, another weakness of the way in which I measured the dependent variable might be that it could be the action of moving between classrooms that affected the dependent variable rather than whether the children learned and recalled more in the same classroom rather than a different classroom. If I reran the experiment I would get the children in condition A to leave their classroom for one minute and then return to their places in the same classroom for recall. This would remove the potentially confounding variable of movement so that the effect of the IV would be measured more reliably.

You would not need to make all these points to gain full marks – and you could make equally valid points to gain marks. Try to assess whether you have enough to gain ten marks.

Self-report procedure

Example 2 (Self-report): In order to investigate students' attitudes to A Level Psychology nationally, I would approach each exam board in the country and ask them to randomly select 1 per cent of centres that had students who take A Level Psychology. These centres would be approached and asked whether the students at their centre would be willing to respond to a questionnaire on how they found studying A Level Psychology, including the syllabus and the teaching they received. Each school would put the names of all their students into a hat and select randomly 10 per cent of their students to fill in the questionnaire. The students would be assured of anonymity and that their responses would be sent directly to the experimenter and would not be seen by their school or by the exam board. Responses could then be analysed and would be representative of students' view nationally of A Level Psychology.

The main strength of this sampling method is that it would be truly representative of A Level Psychology students. This is because using percentages would enable the experimenter to access information from the proportion of students studying Psychology under each different exam board. Moreover, each centre would randomly select a percentage of their students, so again this would ensure a representative sample. A large centre with 300 Psychology students would return questionnaires from 30 randomly selected students whereas a small centre with, say, 20 students studying Psychology would return questionnaires from only two students. Another strength of this procedure is that students could be assured of anonymity, so their responses would not be affected by social desirability factors.

The above is a likely answer, but you could suggest another sampling method and as long as it was clearly explained in enough detail to allow replication and was evaluated for strengths and weaknesses, you could gain full marks.

3.7.5 Calculating measures of central tendency and suggesting appropriate measures of central tendency in relation to source material

A1. The median is a measure of central tendency that is calculated by putting the values in numerical order and finding the middle value in the set. If there are an even number of values (as in this case), you add the two middle values and divide by two to find the middle value. The median value for condition 1 was 8.5 and for condition 2 was 7.5.

A2. To calculate the mean score for participants in each condition, first you would add the scores of participants in each condition, then you would divide by the number of participants in each condition (10). Mean score in condition 1 was 8.1 and in condition 2 was 7.7.

A3. The descriptive statistic called the mode might be appropriate for a study such as that outlined above. This is because when you find the mode you are dealing with whole numbers and looking for the most common value. In this example neither the mean nor the median gives you a whole number, so neither of them is really representative of the scores achieved in each condition. If you find the modal score for each group it will be a whole number and probably representative of scores achieved by several participants. This may be more representative of the data. In this case the modal score in condition 1 is 9 and in condition 2 is 7.

3.7.7 Graphical representations of data

Your graph should look something like this:

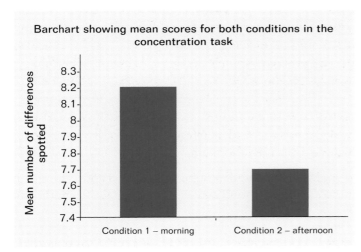

Figure 3.2

A Participants achieved a higher mean score in condition 1 than in condition 2.

Note to students and teachers

Please bear in mind when using these sample questions and answers, that the answers are not designed to be perfect top-band answers. They are to point you in the right direction when you are thinking about how to answer questions in the exam, you will have to use your own knowledge and the guidance in this book, to reach for those top marks.

Part Two
OCR A2 Unit G544: Approaches and Research Methods in Psychology

Chapter 4 Designing a practical
          project   96
Chapter 5 Approaches, perspectives
          and debates for A2   117
Chapter 6 Research methods for A2 141

Introduction

In the second half of this book we will examine in more detail the additional skills and material that you need to cover for the A2 examination paper G544. This paper is synoptic, which means that you will need to be fully prepared on the material in the preceding chapters aimed at AS Level as well as developing your understanding of the new material. When you are asked to give examples of psychological research to support your answers you may refer to both AS Core Studies and studies you have met while studying any of the applied options. This book has been written to accompany the Hodder publications *Psychology AS for OCR*, *Psychology A2 for OCR* and *OCR A2 Psychology Key Studies Companion*. A2 examples cited here will be taken from the Key Studies that are summarised in the latter two books, but in the examination you are encouraged to cite any relevant studies that you know. You will not be familiar with all the examples provided as they are taken from all four of the applied options. You will therefore sometimes need to substitute other examples that you have come across and you should not feel in any way constrained to limit examples to those selected here. However, this book is intended as a useful support for the synoptic paper and will provide guidance in terms of how to use examples of relevant psychological research in your examination responses.

4 Designing a practical project

4.1 Selection and construction of a
    research question   96
Answers   110

The major step up from G541: Psychological Investigations to G544: Approaches and Research Methods in Psychology is the requirement that you design a practical project of your own during the examination and evaluate it. This question is worth approximately 20 per cent of the total exam marks. In G541 sample material is provided that summarises briefly examples of research projects and you are asked to comment on the strengths and weaknesses of the project described. In G544 you are also given some sample material but then you have to design a suitable project that fulfils the stated requirements and is sufficiently detailed and valid to enable you (or someone else) to go ahead and run that project successfully afterwards. This means that you now have to put to the test your understanding of all the issues that have already been covered in the first three chapters of this book, such as sampling, data collection and control of variables. In this chapter we will not go over again in detail any of the material that has already been covered, but will instead focus on how you should design your project, providing additional guidance on those aspects that are new at A2 Level.

4.1 Selection and construction of a research question

Sometimes you will be provided with a research question or choice of research questions to investigate. If you have a choice of research questions you should plan how you would carry out a project to answer each research question before deciding which one to select. Your choice will depend on personal factors. You may have undertaken a practical project in class that resembles one of the options. Alternatively, one question may be of more interest to you than another, or one question may spark more ideas in your mind than another. It should not matter too much which one you choose, but in designing your practical project you must keep focused on the research question and make sure that the project you plan and describe will answer the research question that you have selected.

Here is an examination-style example.

Practical project example A: Memory experiment

Memory is a curious thing. Sometimes there are things we can't forget, however hard we try. Other things that we want to learn just won't stay in our heads! Have you ever had the experience of discussing a past event with a friend or member of your family and you find that you and they have very different memories of the same event? Some people think that we subconsciously block traumatic events. Other people think that therapists who claim that they can recover lost memories have accidentally planted false memories in their patients. There is still a lot that we don't know about how memory works.

Here are some sample research questions that relate to memory:

(a) Does women's memory ability decline after childbirth?
(b) Do men remember facts better than women?
(c) Do women remember personal details such as birthdays better than men?
(d) Is it easier to remember lists of familiar words better than lists of unfamiliar words?

You are required to design a practical project to investigate one of the above research questions. It must be an independent-measures design experiment and you must plan to collect at least ordinal data. It should be a project that you could carry out. You must choose **one** of the options (a) to (d).

State the option from (a) to (d) you have chosen for your practical project

....

Following this there will be a list of questions for you to answer, including a question asking you to describe and evaluate the plan of the practical investigation you would conduct in order to answer the research question you have selected.

4.1.1 Construction of a research question

An alternative approach to the above example is that you may be asked to supply your own research question in response to the source material. A research question is a question that a researcher poses that they wish to investigate. It should relate clearly to the aim of the project as conveyed by the source material.

Here is an examination-style example.

Practical project example B: Investigation of stress

Your task is to answer questions about how a piece of research related to the passage below could be conducted.

A researcher wants to investigate stress levels. There are a number of possible sources of stress in people's lives. One way to find out more about one of these sources of stress and its effects is to ask people to fill out a questionnaire. In this way they can respond in some detail about this aspect of their lives as a potential stressor.

You must choose one of the options (a) to (f).

(a) Job-related stress
(b) Daily hassles
(c) Relationship stress
(d) Financial worries
(e) Health concerns
(f) Concern about crime.

You must design a study that uses a questionnaire to collect data by opportunity sampling.

State the option from (a) to (f) you have chosen for your practical project

....

Q Construct a research question for your practical project. (3 marks)

We will select option (a) job–related stress.

- The task is to construct a research question for a practical project on job–related stress.
- In order to construct a research question you need to identify your aim.
- Our aim could be to investigate how job–related stress affects people in different occupations.
- We now need to frame this as a research question.

A Research question: Do people in some types of jobs feel more stressed than in other types of jobs?

Here is an example for you to have a go at yourself. You will find a likely answer on p.110.

Practical project example C: Memory distortion

Your task is to answer questions about how a piece of research related to the passage below could be conducted.

Cognitive processes like memory can be subject to distortion. Researchers want to run an experiment to find out how various factors can affect or distort memory.

You must choose to investigate one of the variables (a) to (c).

(a) Leading questions
(b) Priming with happy or sad faces
(c) Distractor events.

You must use an independent–samples design and it must be a practical project that could be conducted without breaking ethical guidelines.

State the option from (a) to (c) you have chosen for your practical project

....

Q Construct a research question for your practical project. (3 marks)

4.1.2 Framing operationalised alternate and null hypotheses (one-tailed and two-tailed)

For information on alternate and null hypotheses, please refer back to Chapter 2, p.18.

Now read again Practical project example A: Memory experiment on p.97. Let's decide that we are going to plan a project to investigate research question (a) Does women's memory ability decline after childbirth?

You might first be asked to state the null hypothesis. Remember that the null hypothesis in an experiment is that there will be no effect of the IV on the DV. Another way of expressing the null hypothesis is that there will be no difference in results between the two conditions of the IV.

When you formulate a null hypothesis in the examination you are expected to operationalise it even if the question does not explicitly mention this. This includes the following:

● How you plan to manipulate the IV – which means you must clearly describe both conditions of your experiment

● A clear explanation of exactly how the DV will be measured or scored

You can see that before you can begin to answer these questions you need to plan exactly how you will conduct your practical project. In order to state the null hypothesis you need to identify your IV and DV. In this case our IV is a naturally occurring one (having been through childbirth or not) and the DV will be a measure of memory, for example score on a task where the participant has to memorise 20 word pairs.

Q See whether you can state operationalised null and alternate hypotheses reflecting the research question.

A possible answer for Practical Project A , option a) might be:

A Null hypothesis: There will be no difference in memory ability, as measured by the number of word pairs correctly recalled out of 20, between women who have given birth within the past six months and women who have never given birth.

Alternate hypothesis: Women who have given birth within the past six months will show lower memory ability, as measured by the number of word pairs correctly recalled out of 20, than women who have never given birth.

The above hypothesis is 'one-tailed' that is, it predicts the direction of the difference in memory ability between mothers who have or have not given birth in the past six months.

You could if you prefer formulate a 'two tailed' alternate hypothesis. A two-tailed hypothesis predicts a difference in results between the two groups in the experiment but stays open-minded about which way the difference will go. Which do you think is more appropriate in the above example, a one-tailed or a two-tailed hypothesis?

Could you formulate a suitable two-tailed hypothesis for this example?

Here is another example for you to do. You will find a possible answer on p.110.

Read through Practical Project C: Memory distortion and then answer the following questions in relation to option (a) leading questions.

Q 1. State a one-tailed alternate hypothesis for your practical project. (3 marks)

Q 2. State a null hypothesis for your practical project (3 marks)

Make sure you operationalise both the IV and the DV.

4.1.3 Developing and describing procedure – experiments

You will be asked to describe the method you would use to conduct your practical project. You will be awarded 13 marks for replicability and appropriateness of your design and 6 marks for the quality of the design and its feasibility.

Let's take the example of Practical project example A: Memory experiment. As this is an experiment it is vital that you mention the IV, the DV and controlling variables. You will be given no other guidance so it is very important that you draw a rough plan and try to remember to include all the important steps in conducting a practical project. You may find it helpful to refer to the nine steps described in Chapter 3, p.65–6.

We have already dealt with the research question and we have operationalised the hypothesis, so we can cross off steps 1 and 2, which mean we can begin with step 3 – recruiting the sample, before going on to discuss the IV, allocation of participants to the experimental conditions, stating the DV and how it will be measured. We also need to refer to ethical guidelines.

Here is an example of how this question might be approached with regard to research question (a) Does women's memory ability decline after childbirth? The sample material stated that the design should be independent samples.

Q Describe the method you would use to conduct your practical project. (13 + 6 marks)

A I would obtain a self-selecting sample for this experiment. I would advertise at a doctor's clinic for women volunteers aged 25–35 who had not had children and for women volunteers in the same age group who had given birth to their first child in the past six months. I would try to obtain ten volunteers in each group. This would be a quasi-experiment as the IV is whether the participants have had a baby or not. I would arrange with the permission of the doctor for participants to take a computerised memory test next time they visited the doctor's surgery. Participants would take the test in a quiet room in the surgery. The mothers with babies would be able to bring their child with them into the room. Before giving the participants instructions on taking the test I would obtain informed consent from them. I would then give the participants a list of 20 word pairs, which they would have one minute to learn. Then the participant would take a computerised test in which one of each pair of words on the list would be displayed on the screen and the participant would have to choose the other one of the pair from a choice of four.

After taking the test the participant would be thanked and debriefed. The DV would be the number of correctly identified pairs of words, with the maximum score being 20. The mean score of each group would be calculated and compared to see whether the alternate hypothesis was supported – that is, whether the women who had recently given birth scored less well on the memory test than those who had not had a baby.

You may be able to see some problems in the above method, but that does not matter. As long as the method you suggest is practical and replicable it does not have to be perfect. The next questions will probably ask you to discuss whether an alternative experimental design could have been used, as well as about the validity of your design, representativeness of the sample and ethical issues.

Q Give an advantage of using an alternative design in this practical project. (3 marks)

The question specified that an independent-measures design should be used. Do you think that is the best design to answer the research question?

A Repeated measures could be used in this study. You could test women at an antenatal clinic (a clinic for expectant mothers) in the months before their due date and then you could test the same women a few months after they give birth. The advantage of this is that it would remove participant variables as you would be testing the same people in each condition.

Q Assess the validity of your design in terms of the measurement of the DV. (3 marks)

Validity involves whether you are measuring what you want to measure, the ecological validity of the investigation and the reliability of the measure. This question asks you to focus on the measure of the DV so you need not go into detail on other issues such as the sample.

A This is a valid procedure for testing the effects of childbirth on memory. It uses an independent measures design which avoids practice effects. The measure is reliable because the procedure was standardised and the responses recorded automatically on a computer. The study has face validity because it is a measure of memory ability in women who have not had children and those who have recently had a baby. The measure is an appropriate measure of memory ability, which has fairly high ecological validity as it reflects the kind of memory demands we meet in real life. The women recruited were from the same age group so age is not a confounding variable. However, the women with children had their babies with them when they took the test so this might have affected their ability to concentrate on the memory task and this may affect the validity of the findings.

Q Outline how you might have selected a sample that would have been more representative. (3 marks)

We described a self-selecting sample because this seemed practical in terms of the nature of the study. However, it may not have been representative of the target population.

A A random-sampling technique might have produced a more representative sample than a self-selecting sample. Rather than asking for volunteers I could have asked the doctor to randomly select ten childless women and ten women who had recently had babies out of all the patients on their database. This would have been more representative as all the women registered with the practice who met these conditions would have had an equal chance of being selected. My volunteer sample might have been biased as perhaps women experiencing memory problems might not have volunteered for fear they would do badly on the test.

Q What ethical issues would you consider in designing your practical project? (3 marks)

We already mentioned a couple of ethical issues in our procedure. These can be repeated and any other ethical concerns can be stated.

A I would ensure that all participants gave informed consent and were debriefed. Another ethical issue is whether it is unethical to use a doctor's list and surgery to obtain participants. In this case, though, the findings could have medical implications if the hypothesis that childbirth leads to a decline in memory ability is supported, so this may justify the study. Another ethical issue is that data from all participants should be anonymously recorded.

You might also be asked about changes you would make to your study or implications for future research.

Q Suggest <u>one</u> idea for possible future research related to your practical project. (3 marks)

This gives you the opportunity to think about the wider implications of your study.

A It would be useful to conduct longitudinal research to see whether any memory problems experienced by women within six months of childbirth persist over a longer period or whether women's memory ability a year or two after giving birth is no different from the memory of similar-aged women who have not had children.

We have now explored specimen questions for the whole of section A of G544.

Now see whether you can apply your understanding to answering a similar set of questions with reference to Practical Project example C: Memory distortion. This time we will take option (c) Distractor events (e.g. watching a second video as a distractor before answering a questionnaire). It is again stated that this should be an independent–samples design.

See whether you can design a suitable practical project and answer the following questions. (Likely answers will be found at the end of this chapter, pp.110–12.)

Q 1. Describe the method you would use to conduct your practical project. (13 + 6 marks)

Q 2. Describe <u>one</u> weakness of using an independent-samples design in your investigation. (3 marks)

Q 3. Discuss the validity of your design in terms of the IV and the measurement of the DV. (6 marks)

Q 4. Outline an alternative method that you might have used to select your sample and assess which method would have been more representative. (3 marks)

Q 5. What ethical issues would you consider in designing your practical project? (3 marks)

Q 6. Outline <u>one</u> improvement that you could make to your study. (3 marks)

4.1.4 Developing and describing procedure – self-report investigations

The examples discussed above are both experiments. However, you could equally be asked to describe the procedure for a self-report investigation, a correlation or an observation. You can still apply the nine-steps approach to describing the procedure, but the steps (and questions asked) will be slightly different in each case. In a self-report study there will no operationalised hypotheses, no IV or DV. Instead you will need to provide details of the questionnaire you would construct, paying attention to questions of qualitative and quantitative data, open and closed questions and use of rating scales.

You will again be asked to describe the method you would use to conduct your practical project and you will usually be awarded 13 marks for replicability and appropriateness of your design and 6 marks for the quality of the design and its feasibility.

Let's take the example of Practical project example B: Investigation of stress. See whether on the basis of the guidance provided you can answer the following questions. (Likely answers will be found on pp.112–13.)

Q 1. Describe the method you would use to conduct your practical project. (13+6 marks)

NB: We have already completed step 1 (constructing a research question) so you should move on to step 2 – planning sampling method and construction of questionnaire. You should pay attention to practical questions such as the distribution and collection of your questionnaires as well as the construction of the questionnaire. You should also keep in mind the research question you have constructed – in our case the extent of workplace stress and how it differs in different occupations.

Q 2. Outline one advantage of using a questionnaire in your practical project. (3 marks)

Remember, this is asking you not about the advantages of questionnaires in general but about what it is about your research question that lends itself to study via the self-report method.

Q 3a. Explain one strength of using closed questions in your practical project. (3 marks)

Q 3b. Explain one weakness of using closed questions in your practical project. (3 marks)

Q 4. Explain how using leading questions could influence the results of your practical project. (3 marks)

Q 5. How could you ensure that your questionnaire would not cause too much distress to the participants? (3 marks)

As with the other questions, you should not give a generalised answer here about avoiding psychological harm. You should think about the focus of your questionnaire, why it might cause distress, and how this could be avoided.

Q 6. Suggest a more appropriate sampling method you could have used to obtain participants for your practical project. Explain your answer. (3 marks)

4.1.5 Developing and describing procedure – correlational investigation

In some ways being asked to describe a suitable procedure for a correlational investigation is particularly challenging. This is because correlation is a method of data analysis, not a method of data collection. Don't be put off. But you should pay attention to the source material and from that you should be able to work out what procedure you will need to use in collecting your data. The emphasis in the question will be on data analysis, reflecting the fact that the study is correlational. You can still apply the nine-steps approach to describing the procedure, but the steps (and questions asked) will depend on the type of data you are advised to collect. In a correlational study there will be no operationalised hypotheses, no IV or DV. Instead you will need to focus on relationships between variables and data analysis.

You will again be asked to describe the method you would use to conduct your practical project and you will usually be awarded 13 marks for replicability and appropriateness of your design and 6 marks for the quality of the design and its feasibility.

Here is an example.

Your task is to answer questions about how a piece of research related to the passage below could be conducted. (Likely answers will be found on pp.113–15.)

Psychologists have hypothesised that various factors may be correlated with intelligence, such as visual acuity, working-memory capacity, speed of information processing and reaction time. Correlations between scores on verbal-reasoning tests and scores on a variety of computer tests can be investigated for this question.

You must choose to investigate correlations between verbal reasoning and one of the variables (a) to (d):

(a) Visual perception
(b) Working-memory store
(c) Speed of information processing
(d) Reaction time on a computer.

You must design a practical project that could be conducted using a self-selecting sample of college students. Take option (d) and see whether on the basis of the guidance provided you can answer the following questions:

Q 1. What is your research question? (3 marks)

Remember to discuss relationships, not effects.

Q 2. State an appropriate alternate hypothesis. (3 marks)

Q 3. Describe the method you would use to conduct your practical project. (13+6 marks)

Remember as this is correlational there will be no IV or DV. You must give thought to how you would obtain your sample, how you would collect your data relating to both variables and how you would work out whether there is a relationship between them.

Q 4. Explain why it is more appropriate to study this question using the correlational method rather than an experiment. (3 marks)

Q **5.** Sketch how data you might collect in your study could be showed graphically. (3 marks)

You should draw a scattergraph – remember to label both axes clearly.

Q **6.** What ethical issues would you consider in designing your practical project? (3 marks)

Q **7.** Outline <u>one</u> improvement that you could make to your study. (3 marks)

4.1.6 Developing and describing procedure – observations

Here you will be asked to describe the method you would use to conduct your practical project. You will be awarded 13 marks for replicability and appropriateness of your design and 6 marks for the quality of the design and its feasibility.

You will be given no other guidance so it is very important that you draw a rough plan and try to remember to include all the important steps in conducting an observation. You may find it helpful to refer to the nine steps described in Chapter 3, p.65–6.

As this is an observation there will no operationalised hypotheses, no IV or DV. Instead you will need to focus on the practical issues involved in planning and running an observation. Here is an example. (Likely answers will be found on pp.115–16.)

Your task is to answer questions about how a piece of research related to the passage below could be conducted.

Social psychologists have noted that some people take a dominant role in group contexts. The nature of this domination will depend on the context in which the group is operating. One way to find out more about group dynamics is to run an observational investigation.

You must choose between the different group contexts listed below (a) to (d):

(a) A group of young people drinking in a pub
(b) A football team in training
(c) A business board meeting
(d) A group of children playing in a school playground.

You must design a practical project that could be conducted. This should be an overt observation.

Take option (c) and see whether on the basis of the guidance provided you can answer the following questions.

Q **1.** Describe the method you would use to conduct your practical project. (13 + 6 marks)

You will need to focus on devising a suitable observation schedule and deciding details like whether to use time sampling or event sampling, how many observers you would use and what types of behaviours you would record.

Q **2.** Explain the difference between an overt and a covert observation and outline a strength of using an overt observation in your practical investigation. (3 marks)

Q **3.** Outline one strength and one weakness of time sampling in the context of your practical investigation. (6 marks)

Q **4.** What ethical issues would you consider in designing your practical project? (3 marks)

Q **5.** Outline <u>one</u> improvement that you could make to your study. (3 marks)

4.1.7 Further guidance on data: levels of measurement

Just about everything that you have been asked to do in response to the questions relating to section A of G544 discussed up to this point is covered in Chapters 2–3 of this book. However, there are a few additional points relating to data and statistical tests that we need to cover briefly. The sample material on which you are asked to base your method often specifies certain basics. These include experimental design (independent samples, repeated measures or matched participants), type of study (e.g. questionnaire) or approach (e.g. covert observation). The other basic guideline that you may need to meet is the level of the data to be collected. There are four different kinds of scales or levels of measurement:

- Nominal
- Ordinal
- Interval
- Ratio.

Each of these will be discussed briefly in turn.

Nominal data

In nominal data the number is just a label or name for a category that does not have any mathematical properties. For example, you might conduct research to see whether males and females who go into a shop come out with a bag showing that they have purchased an item. This can be coded using the numbers 1 (standing for having made no purchase) and 2 (having made a purchase). You can calculate purchasing frequency for each gender from your nominal data, but the numbers themselves are simply an easy way of coding behaviours.

Ordinal data

If the practical project that you are asked to design is an experiment or a correlation it is likely that the source material will state that you need to collect 'at least ordinal data'. Ordinal data involves numbers that can be put in order but do not have any other mathematical properties. For example, viewers of *X Factor* might be asked to rank the top ten finalists in their preferred order, with their favourite being ranked 10. This would give each finalist a number, but there would be no reality to those numbers. The finalist ranked top (1) would not be measurably twice as popular as the finalist ranked 5. In psychological research most studies that use self-report collect ordinal data as participants are often asked to rank things on a scale of 1–5, but the numbers stand for words such as 'strongly agree' or 'disagree' and do not have any true mathematical relationship to each other. The reason that the source material may ask for 'at least ordinal data' is that ordinal data allow you to calculate measures of central tendency (averages) and measures of dispersion.

If you need to refresh your memory on measures of central tendency and dispersion, see Chapter 3, p.75.

Interval-level data

While the ranks ascribed in ordinal-level data have no true mathematical relationship, interval-level data are data in which the points are evenly spaced. For example, the difference between shoe size 3 and shoe size 4 is the same as between shoe size 4 and shoe size 5. However, there is no zero in shoe sizes so the relationship is relative.

Ratio data

Ratio data are the highest, most precise level of measurement. Unlike interval-level data, zero truly means zero. Often interval and ratio data are grouped together and the question will ask for 'at least interval-level data'. These include physiological measures such as height and weight, but in psychology they also include measures such as scores on an IQ test, number of words remembered in a memory test or time taken to complete a task.

4.1.8 Further guidance on data: inferential tests

The other aspect of data handling that is new at A2 Level is inferential statistics. Inferential tests sound very difficult to the non-mathematically inclined, but no one should be put off from doing A2 Psychology because they are frightened by the sound of inferential statistics. The examiners expect you to have a very basic understanding of the concepts and you are not required to conduct any tests yourself. In this section we will discuss only what you need to know for G544 and no more, so as not to daunt you with statistics. If you are keen to find out more there are plenty of resources available online or in textbooks of research methods and statistics for psychology.

Inferential tests are simply tests that enable us to conclude that a difference we have found between scores of different groups of participants are meaningful (statistically significant) or whether the differences were at a level that may have occurred by chance. An inferential test helps us to decide by working out the probability of whether the difference between the two sets of scores is due to chance or a real effect.

(a) Probability

What you need to know for G544 is how probability is expressed in psychological research and at what level of probability researchers would agree that a finding is not due to chance.

The probability of a difference between groups being due to chance is expressed as $p \leq 0.05$. This means there is 5% or lower probability that the differences are due to chance factors and that there is a 95% or higher probability that the differences are due to the effect of the manipulation of the IV. At this point we can accept that the difference is significant, which means we can reject the null hypothesis and accept the alternate hypothesis. Sometimes psychology researchers want to set a more stringent level of significance, in which case they will set the level at $p \leq 0.01$. This means that the probability that the difference is due to chance factors is only 1% or less and the probability that the finding is due to manipulation of the IV is 99% or higher.

In the examination you will not have to work out levels of significance but you may need to show that you understand them. For example, you may be asked to explain what is meant by the statement 'the researchers set the probability level at $p \leq 0.05$'.

(b) Type 1 and Type 2 errors

Normally we can be confident in accepting the alternate hypothesis when there is a 5% or lower probability of results having occurred by chance. However, we are dealing with probabilities, not with certainties, and sometimes mistakes are made. If we accidentally accept the alternate hypothesis wrongly this may mean that we have not operated a stringent enough measure of probability. This is a false positive or Type 1 error.

If, however, we reject the alternate hypothesis and wrongly accept the null hypothesis, this means that we have operated too stringent a level of probability and the result is a false negative or Type 2 error (see Table 4.1).

Table 4.1 Type 1 and Type 2 errors

| Type 1 error | False positive | Accepting the alternate hypothesis although the null was true |
| Type 2 error | False negative | Accepting the null hypothesis although the alternate was true |

Usually it is important in psychological research that we do not claim the alternate hypothesis is true if it isn't (a false positive) and that is why psychologists sometimes operate on more stringent levels of probability ($p \leq 0.01$).

Types of inferential test

You do not need to know how to carry out inferential tests for G544. However, you may be asked to indicate in relation to designing a procedure which test you would carry out and why.

There are five statistical tests that you need to know about. These are all non–parametric tests. This means that they are tests for data that are not normally distributed.

Extend Your Understanding

Data such as height are normally distributed in the population. This means that when you plot frequency scores on a graph, the data would be bell shaped (see below). This is because the vast majority of the population are around 'average' height and as you move further away from average, the frequency of scores drops rapidly.

You are not asked to understand normal distribution at A2 Level because the majority of psychological research uses a small number of participants and deals with data that are known or presumed not to be normally distributed.

Non-parametric tests (see Table 4.2) are used on data that are either:

● not normally distributed

● not of 'at least interval level', i.e. they are nominal or ordinal data (see p.106).

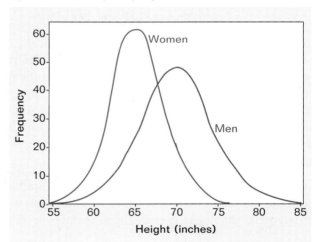

Figure 4.1

Table 4.2 Non-parametric inferential tests and their use

Test	When to use the test
Chi-square test	This is used for nominal data when data are categorical. You can have a two-by-two or a three-by-two chi square test.
Sign test	This is used for ordinal data when you are looking for a difference between conditions and your design is repeated measures. Usually the Wilcoxon is preferred.
Wilcoxon signed-ranks test	This is used for ordinal- or interval-level data and is used when you are looking for a difference between two conditions and when your experimental design is either repeated measures or matched pairs.
Mann-Whitney U test	This is used for ordinal- or interval-level data when you are looking for a difference between two conditions and your experimental design is independent measures.
Spearman's rho rank correlation coefficient	This is a test of relationship (correlation) and can be used for ordinal- or interval-level data and measures relationships between variables for each participant.

In the examination, if you are asked to identify a suitable non–parametric test of significance (inferential test) in relation to your practical project you need to identify:

(a) whether you are testing for difference between groups or scores or for a relationship between variables

(b) whether your experimental design is independent groups or repeated measures/matched participants

(c) whether your data are nominal or ordinal/interval.

If you answer these questions correctly and you learn Table 4.2, you should have no problem identifying the correct test.

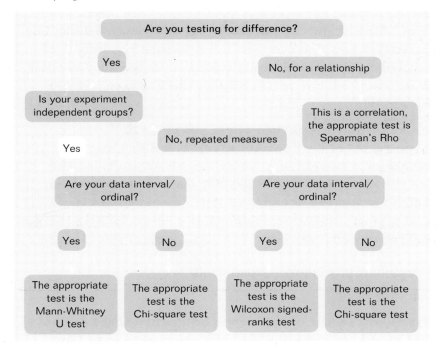

Figure 4.2

Answers

4.1.1 Construction of a research question

Here are likely questions relating to each variable.

- Leading questions

A. To what extent can leading questions asked after an event distort recall of that event?

- Priming with happy or sad faces

A. To what extent does priming with happy or sad faces affect participants' subsequent recall in a memory test of a list of emotionally salient words?

- Distractors

A. To what extent does the presence of a distracting factor (such as a weapon) affect recall of an event?

4.1.2 Framing operationalised alternate and null hypotheses (one-tailed and two-tailed)

Memory distortion – leading questions

A1. An operationalised one-tailed alternate hypothesis is that there will be a difference in recalled estimated height of a perpetrator shown on a video of a mock crime scene, between responses of participants asked a leading question and those not asked a leading question. Participants asked the question 'What height do you think the taller man holding the gun was? 5ft–5ft 5ins/5ft 6ins–6ft/over 6ft' will estimate the height of the perpetrator as taller than participants asked a non-leading question, e.g. 'What height do you think the person holding the gun was? 5ft–5ft 5ins/5ft 6ins–6ft/over 6ft?'

A2. An operationalised null hypothesis is that there will be no difference in recall between responses of participants asked a leading question concerning the height of a suspect, e.g. 'What height do you think the taller man holding the gun was? 5ft–5ft 5ins/5ft 6ins–6ft/over 6ft', as shown in a video of a mock crime scene, and participants asked a non-leading question, e.g. 'What height do you think the person holding the gun was? 5ft–5ft 5ins/5ft 6ins–6ft/over 6ft'.

4.1.3 Developing and describing procedure – experiments

Memory distortion – distractor events

A1. I would use an opportunity sample of sixth-form college students. I would obtain 20 students by asking around in the college common room. The students would be randomly allocated to one of two conditions – with or without a distractor task. The IV would be distractor task or no distractor task. I would conduct the experiment in a classroom. I would ask for informed consent from all participants before starting the experiment. I would show both groups of participants a video clip of a crime scene from a TV programme. In the non-distractor condition I would wait ten minutes after the clip ended and then give the participants a questionnaire to respond to with questions about the crime scene. In the second condition I would show the participants a ten-minute clip from a different TV programme. This would not feature a crime scene but it would be an exciting clip of a car chase. After the participants watched the second film I would give them the same questionnaire about the first film that the participants in the other condition responded to. The questionnaire would contain 20 questions asking about details of the crime scene, the clothing and physical appearance of the criminal and the sequence of events. The dependent variable would be how many of the questions the participant answered correctly.

I would thank and debrief the participants. I would then calculate mean group score on the questionnaire to see whether the hypothesis that the distractor event would distort memory was supported.

A2. One weakness of using an independent-samples design in this experiment is that one group of participants might happen by chance to have better memories than the other group and this would affect the results.

A3. I think this would be a valid design in terms of the IV because people who witnessed a crime would be quite likely to experience other events before having a chance to recall the details to the police, so this study would be quite high in ecological validity. I think that the measure of the DV is valid and reliable because all the participants watched the same video clip and answered the same questionnaire.

A4. I could have obtained a random sample by randomly generating the names of 20 students from a database containing the names of all the students at the college. This would have been representative of the target population (students at the college) because every student would have had an equal chance of being picked.

A5. In designing my project I would have ensured that all participants gave informed consent and were debriefed. I could have ensured that I did not cause psychological harm by checking in advance whether any of the participants had been involved as victims of a crime as this might cause them trauma by making them relive the experience.

A6. One improvement I would make to my study would be to ask participants to return one week later to respond to another set of questions concerning the video clip of the crime. This would test whether the effects of an immediate distractor would still be significant after a longer passage of time.

4.1.4 Developing and describing procedure – self-report investigations

A1. I would first identify my target population. This would be people working in a variety of different types of jobs, e.g. college lecturers, shop assistants, firemen, factory workers. I would identify a local employer in each category and contact them and ask permission to use their email network to send out my questionnaire to obtain an opportunity sample. I would tell the employers that all responses would be anonymous but that I would feed back a summary of my results. I would construct my questionnaire in a way that would enable me to gain answers to critical questions concerning stress, but I would also ask lots of other questions about their work situation so that I would understand the jobs participants did and also so that the participants would not be aware that it was stress I was interested in (to avoid demand characteristics).

I would use mainly closed questions so that the data could be easily analysed and responses compared. However, I would also add some open questions so that participants would be free to write about whatever they wanted to in terms of their feelings about their jobs. For the closed statements I would use a Likert scale of 1–5 where 1 = never and 5 = always. Statements on stress would include the following: I find that I look forward to going into work – circle on a scale of 1 (never) to 5 (always) and I feel very anxious in the mornings before I go into work (circle on a scale of 1 (never) to 5(always). For the open questions I would ask things like 'Identify one aspect of your work that you find particularly satisfying and explain briefly why' and 'Identify one aspect of your work that you find particularly stressful and explain briefly why'. I would give participants a deadline for returning their filled-in questionnaires to me.

Participation would be voluntary. After the deadline had passed I would send an email debriefing participants and telling them that they could read my report once I had completed it. I would then collate the data. The data from the closed statements could be easily analysed and comparisons made between different types of work and stress levels. With the open questions I would code them for similar themes and would then try to make meaningful comparisons between the responses.

A2. An advantage of using a questionnaire in this project on stress is that it is one of the only ways of finding out about stress, the other way being a physiological measure (e.g. saliva for cortisol). A physiological measure would be useful but it would not give you the insights into why people felt stressed that you would gain with a self-report investigation.

A3a. A strength of using closed questions in my practical project is that it would allow me to make comparisons easily between a large number of respondents in different types of employment. This would allow me to calculate whether some jobs appear more stressful than others.

A3b. A weakness of only using closed questions in my practical project would be that they would not give participants the opportunity to pinpoint what they saw as the main cause of stress for them – this might differ a lot from person to person and all potential responses might not be covered by closed categories.

A4. Asking leading questions might bias my results. For example, if I asked outright similar leading questions like 'How stressful do you find your job?' this might lead a participant to think of their job as stressful. However, in my practical project I would counterbalance questions that were asked so that some were positively phrased and others negatively phrased, e.g. I feel stressed before I start work in the morning and I do not feel stressed before I start work in the morning.

A5. It could be quite difficult to ensure that no distress would be caused to participants as someone who was feeling really stressed by their job might find the questionnaire upsetting. I think that although I could not completely avoid this risk I could include a statement at the end of the questionnaire to the effect that if anyone felt upset about their answers and worried about things at work they should think about going to a doctor for advice.

A6. I think that in this case an opportunity sample would be quite appropriate as hopefully the questionnaire would be distributed to a wide range of people in the different workplaces that agreed to participate. However, as I only approached a limited number of workplaces, the target population was not that representative of the whole population of working people. It would have been more representative to send the questionnaire, for example, to every tenth household on the polling register (a systematic sample). This would enable me to find out information about a far wider range of jobs and would be more representative of the whole population.

4.1.5 Developing and describing procedure – correlational investigation

A1. Is there a relationship between verbal reasoning ability and reaction time?

A2. That the higher participants score in verbal-reasoning tests, the quicker they will respond to a stimulus in a reaction-time test.

A3. I would first prepare my materials. These would be a standard computer-administered verbal-reasoning test and a computer test of reaction time (finding a moving target on a computer screen). I would obtain a self-selecting sample from my local college. I would advertise that I wanted people to participate in an experiment that involved playing a game on a computer and taking a computerised test. I would arrange for participants to take the tests individually on my laptop in their free time. Before they took the tests I would assure them of anonymity and explain that I was interested in examining how good people were at computer games. Each participant would first take a 30-minute on-screen verbal-reasoning test. Each participant would also take the moving-target test. The computer would automatically measure the time that elapsed before appearance of a moving-target and the participant 'catching' the target with the mouse. Each participant would have 30 turns at this reaction time test.

I would thank and debrief the participants and would tell them that if they wished they could receive their scores after the project was finished. When all the participants had completed the tasks I would plot their results on both tests and examine the data to see whether there was a correlation.

A4. It is more appropriate to study this question using the correlational method because psychologists do not think that having a high IQ causes you to have a fast reaction time or that having a fast reaction time causes you to have a high IQ. They think that scores in both tests may reflect an underlying general ability and if this is the case scores should be highly correlated.

A5.

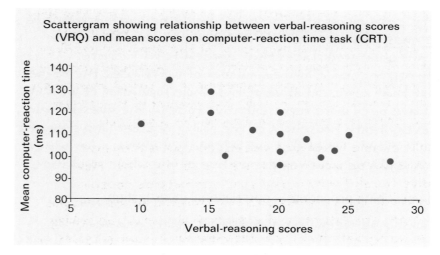

Figure 4.3

A6. Ethical issues I would consider are informed consent and debrief. I might consider not telling the participants what it was about (deception) but would reject that on ethical grounds. I would keep the scores anonymous in handling the data but would give participants a code word so they could access their own results later if they wanted to. An ethical issue here would be that participants with low scores might be upset.

A7. One improvement I would make would be to try to obtain a random sample, which would have been more representative of the target population (all the college students) as each one would have an equal chance of being picked. I used a volunteer sample and stated that this was a computer-based study so I may have attracted people who are very familiar with reaction time-type computer games and therefore they might have been a biased sample.

4.1.6 Developing and describing procedure – observations

A1. I would first of all arrange to conduct my observation. This would be an overt observation so I could contact local businesses and explain my study and ask permission to observe the next meeting of the board that runs the company. I would then devise an appropriate observational schedule. As my research question is about group dynamics and the role of dominant personalities, I would need to draw up a schedule that would enable me to categorise relevant behaviours effectively. I would do a structured sample as in a meeting there would not be time to make detailed qualitative observations. I would probably event sample. I would spend the first five minutes of the meeting deciding who was the dominant personality (or there might be more than one). I would propose to keep a tally of how many times the dominant person spoke and try to categorise the length of what they said each time, e.g. just a short comment; talking for a couple of minutes; holding the floor for a long time. I would also keep a tally of other relevant behaviours, e.g. how often the next speaker agreed with or disagreed with the dominant speaker. I would keep a tally of other people's reactions to the dominant person — how often people nodded their heads in agreement or looked away from the person speaking. I would also try to tally the number of times that each of the other people present contributed to the discussion.

I would have a column free to add comments not covered by my predetermined categories. I would only have one observer as I think it would be intrusive to ask for more than one person to be observing the meeting. I would ask the company boss to introduce me as someone researching boardroom procedures and explain that I would be taking notes during the meeting but that my notes were for my own purposes and that the details under discussion would remain confidential.

A2. A covert observation is an undercover observation where the people being observed do not know that this is being done. An overt observation is one where participants are aware that they are being observed. The advantage of an overt observation in the context of my study is purely practical – it would be impossible to run a covert observation of a boardroom discussion as these meetings are highly confidential.

A3. I decided to event sample in my investigation. A strength of time sampling is richness of data. I could have noted the behaviours of every person in the room at regular intervals during the meeting. I could have numbered each person before I started and then during each minute I could have ticked off what each was doing during that time. This would have given me a more complete picture of all behaviours than event sampling. However, a weakness of time sampling in this context is that there was only one observer (for confidentiality and intrusiveness reasons) and it would have been very difficult in practice to be accurate in time sampling as it would have spread the attention of the observer too widely.

A4. One of the ethical issues in my project is that although I would have had to obtain the informed consent of the company boss, he would probably not have asked for consent of his board members, so I would not have obtained informed consent from all participants. Another ethical issue is the debrief as again this would probably be made to the company boss rather than to all the individuals present (depending how open the company practices were). As these things would not be in my control I could at least make my observations of people's behaviours anonymous so that their privacy could be ensured.

A5. It is always better to have two observers so that accuracy of observations can be assessed using inter-observer reliability checks. Even though it would have been intrusive to have two observers present at a board meeting I think that the gains of doing so would have outweighed the limitations.

Note to students and teachers

Please bear in mind when using these sample questions and answers, that the answers are not designed to be perfect top-band answers. They are to point you in the right direction when you are thinking about how to answer questions in the exam, you will have to use your own knowledge and the guidance in this book, to reach for those top marks.

The previous chapter took you through what you need for answering section A questions of the examination unit G544. This chapter and the following one will take you through what you need to cover in order to be able to answer section B questions of G544. You have a choice of two questions: normally one is on approaches, perspectives and debates and the other on research methods and issues. Some of the questions asked in this section are quite similar to those asked in section C of G542, the Core Studies, but they require responses in more depth and to be supported by more examples. For the basics about the main approaches and perspectives you should return to the material in Chapter 1 of this book as this will not be revisited here. Instead in this chapter we will address the key questions asked in this section and provide a range of examples from the A2 options, as well as summarising the debates.

5.1 Format of section B (Approaches, perspectives and debates) 118

5.2 Forensic Psychology examples: approaches and perspectives 119

5.3 Health and Clinical Psychology examples: approaches and perspectives 121

5.4 Sport and Exercise Psychology examples: approaches and perspectives 123

5.5 Psychology of Education examples: approaches and perspectives 126

5.6 Debates in psychology 128

5.7 Using your knowledge in Unit G544 130

Table 5.1a Approaches and perspectives

Approaches and perspectives
Cognitive
Physiological
Developmental
Social
Individual differences
Behaviourist
Psychodynamic

Table 5.1b Debates

Debates
Determinism/free will
Reductionism/holism
Nature/nurture
Individual/situational
Ethnocentrism
Is psychology a science?
Usefulness of psychology research

5.1 Format of section B (Approaches, perspectives and debates)

This section of the exam usually follows a very similar format. You are required to answer one five-part question. Parts (a)–(e) are worth 40 marks in total and all parts of this question are compulsory (with no choices) if you choose to answer it. The five parts will all relate primarily to one approach or perspective. However in part (d) of this section you will probably be asked to compare the approach that is the focus of the questions with a second, specified approach. Part (e) will probably link up with one debate. Parts (a)–(b) require factual knowledge only, while parts (c)–(e) require you to make evaluative points.

Here are examples based on the cognitive approach and the psychology as science debate:

(a) Using your knowledge of psychology briefly outline the cognitive approach. (4 marks)
(b) Describe two pieces of research that use the cognitive approach. (8 marks)
(c) Discuss the strengths and limitations of using the cognitive approach to explain behaviour. Use examples of psychological research to support your answer. (12 marks)
(d) Compare the cognitive approach to the behaviourist perspective. Use examples of psychological research to support your answer. (8 marks)
(e) Discuss aspects of the cognitive approach that support the argument that psychology is a science. (8 marks)

You may use AS studies only in your answers if you wish but the examiners would prefer you to show knowledge of A2 studies as well, and you will definitely be in a better position to answer some questions if you can draw on your A2 knowledge as well as the AS Core Studies. Before going on to give guidance on how to answer the questions we will turn first to A2 studies from each of the applied options that you might find useful for this section. The examples given here are studies selected as key studies in the accompanying textbook *Psychology A2 for OCR*. These are indicative of the studies you might wish to refer to. You should not feel restricted in any way to the examples shown here. For your guidance the respective section and subsection details are given as it is likely that any alternative studies used in the same section will be useful.

5.2 Forensic Psychology examples: approaches and perspectives

Cognitive approach

Forensic Psychology is rich in cognitive-approach studies. There are examples you can use in all four sections of this option.

Loftus, Loftus and Messo (1987) conducted an independent-samples experiment to investigate the effect of a weapon on participants' recall of a crime scene seen on a series of slides. The scene was a check-out at a fast food outlet. In one condition a customer was shown paying a cheque and in the other the customer was shown drawing a gun on the cashier. Participants were 80 psychology students. The participants watched the slides then responded to a questionnaire. They were then offered pictures of 12 people and were asked to identify the person involved. Loftus, Loftus and Messo found that participants in the weapon condition were significantly less accurate in responding to the questionnaire and in making identification from the line-up than controls. Participants were correct on 56 per cent of the questionnaire items while control participants were correct on 67 per cent of the items. On the 12-person line-up participants in the weapon condition were correct only 15 per cent of the time, while control participants were correct 35 per cent of the time.

(Making a Case 1.2, Factors influencing identification)

Physiological approach

There are fewer physiological studies described in Forensic Psychology but you still have some choice. Look in particular at the sections Turning to Crime (Biological) and After a Guilty Verdict.

Raine, Buchsbaum and LaCasse (1997) conducted an investigation using PET scans to identify differences in brain activation of murderers who had pleaded not guilty due to insanity as compared to the brains of non-murderers. They found reduced activation in the prefrontal areas (implicated in violence) and the corpus callosum (that links the left and right hemispheres), reduced activity in several left-hemisphere areas including left amygdale and left hippocampus and greater activation in the right amygdale and right hippocampus. The study provided preliminary evidence that murderers who have pleaded not guilty by reason of insanity have different brain functioning from normal controls. The data provide some general support for pre-existing biological theories of violence. However, the data were correlational so cause and effect cannot be proved.

(Turning to Crime 3.1, Brain dysfunction)

Social approach

Forensic Psychology can offer a number of useful social-approach studies. Dealing with crime and offending behaviour are processes that are shaped by human interactions. You should be able to find examples of social-approach studies from all four sections of Forensic Psychology.

Social psychologists are particularly interested in group dynamics. A good example of a forensic psychology social-approach study is **Clark (1998)**, which is an examination of the effect of minority influence on jury decision making. This was an independent-measures experiment using 270 students as participants. Participants were asked to read an account of a real first-degree murder case, in which a young man was accused of murdering his father, focusing on the jury deliberations. The IV was different versions of the jury discussions, in some of which a minority jury member consistently refuted the evidence against the defendant. It was found that participants were more influenced by the minority when it provided persuasive arguments by refuting the majority viewpoint than when the minority simply argued against guilt without refuting the evidence. More minority influence occurred when the minority obtained majority defectors.

(Reaching a Verdict 3.3, Minority influence)

Individual-differences approach

There are not many studies in Forensic Psychology that adopt a primarily individual-differences approach. However, several studies identify individual differences as one important factor among others in explaining issues such as why people turn to crime or whether offenders have different thinking patterns from non-offenders (e.g. Juby and Farrington, 2001; Wikström, 2003 and Gudjonsson and Sigurdsson, 2007).

Palmer and Connelly (2005) is a study of depression and suicides among offenders in prison. Palmer and Connelly in this study have sought to move the emphasis away from individual differences alone (i.e. that such events are simply the outcome of mental illness) to a broader explanatory framework that highlights ways in which the prison environment can lead offenders to feel a sense of hopelessness and to experience suicidal ideation. However the authors recognise that individual differences matter and that some individuals are resilient to the pressures of prison life while others are very vulnerable. They explore the links between self-harming, depression and suicide and argue that vulnerable prisoners should be identified so that they can be watched carefully for signs that they may be at risk.

(After a Guilty Verdict 1.2, Depression/suicide risk in jail)

Developmental approach

The Forensic Psychology option is a useful one to refer to in answering developmental questions as the majority of studies referred to in Turning to Crime are developmental. Some of them may be classified under a different approach, but you can still use them here. That is because developmental psychology refers to research that focuses on changes over the life span. It is not a methodological approach. Developmental research therefore is normally from the cognitive or physiological approach as well as being developmental. An example of this from AS is Samuel and Bryant (1983) which is both cognitive and developmental.

Chen and Howitt (2007) is an investigation into moral reasoning in young offenders. They compared moral reasoning ability in hundreds of young offenders in Taiwan with moral reasoning of young people in high schools in Taiwan. They found that the developmental level of moral reasoning was significantly lower in the offender population than in the normal population. This relates to Kohlberg's model of moral development in which he theorised that there are different stages of moral development just as there are different stages of cognitive development.

(Turning to Crime 2.2, Moral development and crime)

Behaviourist perspective

There are not as many Forensic Psychology studies that are behaviourist in approach.

Sutherland's differential association theory or Bandura's Social Learning Theory may be cited here. **Akers *et al*. (1979)** is a study that used self-report to test both these behavioural theories in explaining illegal drinking and drug-habit patterns among 2,500 adolescents from mid-western America. The study found that differential association (and particularly associations with peers) was the factor that explained most of the variance in behaviour. This means that the more young people associate with others who drink and take drugs (especially friends of the same age) the more likely they are to fall into the same habits.

(Turning to Crime 1.2, Learning from others)

Psychodynamic perspective

There are no Forensic Psychology studies suggested in the OCR specification that have a psychodynamic perspective. You would be well advised to stick with AS studies Freud and Thigpen and Cleckley.

5.3 Health and Clinical Psychology examples: approaches and perspectives

Cognitive approach

There are many examples of cognitive-approach studies in Health and Clinical Psychology. Some of them focus on models such as the Health Belief Model and Bandura's theory of self-efficacy or they deal with cognitive explanations for, and treatments of, psychological disorders.

Zalewska-Puchala *et al*. (2007) conducted a survey of college students to examine self-efficacy and the relationship (correlation) between self-efficacy and health behaviours, with 164 nursing students at two Polish universities responding to two self-report measures. One was a self-efficacy scale and one was a study of health-related behaviours e.g. diet, alcohol consumption, etc. Participants' BMI was also measured. Most participants were found to be underweight. Most were found to have high self-efficacy. Most participants reported that they limited fat intake but that they did not ensure that they ate enough fibre. Most participants did not smoke but most did report regular drinking of alcohol. Most participants reported that they took regular exercise. This study showed a relationship between feelings of being in control (self-efficacy) and adoption of a generally healthy lifestyle. However, this appeared to be more to do with the desire to be physically attractive than for health reasons as self-efficacy was positively correlated with alcohol consumption and was correlated to low fat intake but not to fibre intake.

(Healthy Living 1.3, Self-efficacy)

Physiological approach

There are naturally many physiological-approach studies in Health and Clinical Psychology as this is the applied option that is most closely allied to medicine. You may cite here any studies that use physiological measures (e.g. measures of medical adherence or stress) or those that explore physiological bases for psychological disorders.

Kendler *et al*. (1991) is a study of more than 1,000 female twin pairs that aimed to investigate the major risk factors for the eating disorder, bulimia nervosa. This was a self-report study that was conducted using personal structured interviews. Dizygotic and monozygotic twin pairs were compared. Participants were asked questions about weight, exercise and body image. About 3 per cent were found to suffer from bulimia. Methods used to control weight gain were primarily exercise followed by strict dieting and self-induced vomiting. Various risk factors were identified and it was found that the risk in a monozygotic co-twin of an affected twin was more than eight times the risk found in the general population. This shows a clearly identified genetic (physiological) component in bulimia.

(Dysfunctional behaviour 2.2, Biological explanations)

Social approach

There are not many social-approach studies in Health and Clinical Psychology as the majority of studies are from a cognitive, physiological or behaviourist approach. The study cited below is a combination of cognitive and social psychology.

Sinha, Nayyar and Sinha (2002) investigated the effects of social support and self-control in older adults in India. This was a self-report study carried out among 300 adults aged 60+ who live in Agra, India. The participants lived in extended families in high-density households. Participants were assessed using various self-report measures including a measure of social support. The study found that social support acted as an important buffer protecting older adults from stress and loss of control. They recommended that providing social support and enhancing self-efficacy are intervention strategies that can be used to enhance older people's perceived control and to change negative attitudes to life and improve life satisfaction.

(Stress 3.3, Social approaches)

Individual-differences approach

You will recall that all the individual differences Core Studies relate to psychological dysfunction (diagnosis of psychological disorders, multiple personality disorder and addiction). It will therefore come as no surprise to find that you will have a lot of choice in answering on the individual-differences approach in relation to Health and Clinical Psychology. As is the case with the developmental approach, individual differences does not have its own research methodology but can involve a mixture of cognitive and physiological measures in identifying individual differences. In answering on this approach you can refer to classification systems for mental illnesses or differences in cognitive style between individuals with disorders and healthy individuals.

Lewinsohn et al. (1980) is a study that highlights individual differences in self-perception between individuals with depression and healthy individuals. Rather than finding that those with depression are characterised by over-negative cognitions they found that 'normal' people have their self-esteem protected by an over-positive self-image, while people with depression have a more realistic (i.e. more negative) self-image that is more in line with other people's views of them.

(Disorders 2.3, Cognitive explanations of depression)

Developmental approach

There are very few studies in Health and Clinical Psychology that are specifically developmental, however there is information relating to development in several sections of this option. Adolescence and young adulthood and old age are periods when individuals are particularly prone to develop dysfunctional behaviours. One study that looks specifically at psychological disorders in childhood and their treatment is **Whittington et al. (2004)**.

Whittington et al. (2004) is a review of research on the efficacy of SSRIs (selective serotonin reuptake inhibitors) as a treatment for depression in childhood. The study examined both published and unpublished data from several studies and came to the important conclusion that most SSRI medications prescribed have not only proved ineffective in reducing symptoms of depression but have actually raised the risk of suicidal ideation and 'severe adverse events' (e.g. suicide attempts) among children to whom these drugs have been prescribed. The only SSRI to come out of this review with reasonably positive recommendation is fluoxetine.

(Dysfunctional Behaviour 3.2, Biological treatments)

Behaviourist perspective

The behaviourist perspective is very thoroughly covered in Health and Clinical Psychology so there is a wealth of studies to choose from.

Watson and Rayner (1920) is a classic study of emotional conditioning of a phobia in a small child. Watson and Rayner used classical conditioning techniques to associate a loud, unpleasant noise (an unconditioned stimulus) with a furry stimulus such as a white rat that initially was not feared by the baby boy but which Little Albert was conditioned to fear through the association with the loud noise. Watson and Rayner initially intended studying the process of removal of a phobia by trying to reduce Little Albert's fear of the white rat but the baby was removed from the hospital (and hence the study) before they were able to test their approach. Nevertheless generations of clinical psychologists have applied behaviourist theory in order to help patients overcome phobias.

(Dysfunctional Behaviour 2.1, Behavioural explanations)

Psychodynamic perspective

Although many therapists and clinical psychologists use psychodynamic techniques in treating clients the OCR specification does not include psychodynamic studies in Health and Clinical Psychology so you may need to refer to AS Core Studies Freud and Thigpen and Cleckley.

5.4 Sport and Exercise Psychology examples: approaches and perspectives

Cognitive approach

In Sport and Exercise Psychology there are many examples of cognitive theories and studies that employ the cognitive approach. You may refer to theories of arousal, anxiety, self-confidence and motivation as these all engage cognitive processes.

Munroe-Chandler, Hall and Fishbourne (2008) conducted a study to examine the relationship between mental imagery and confidence in soccer players. This was a correlational study involving over 120 Canadian junior athletes. The Sport Imagery Questionnaire for Children was used, which measured frequency of children's imagery use on a five-point scale where 1 = not at all and 5 = very often. The questionnaire contained statements relating to each of five aspects of imagery like 'I can usually control how a skill looks in my head'. The CSAI-2 was administered to assess confidence and a self-efficacy measure was also administered. The authors found that imagery was a significant predictor of both self-confidence and self-efficacy in soccer players. They concluded that young athletes who want to increase their self-confidence should engage more in imagery techniques.

(Sport Performance 3.3, Imagery)

Physiological approach

To date not many studies in Sport and Exercise Psychology have employed the physiological approach, but the use of scanning technology to investigate questions of interest to sports and exercise psychologists is likely to increase.

Bernstein *et al*. (1994) investigated correlations between regular exercise and breast cancer in young women. This was a matched-pairs design in which 545 women newly diagnosed with breast cancer were age-matched and neighbourhood-matched with healthy controls. Participants were individually reviewed, medical histories taken, and lifetime history of regular participation in physical exercise recorded, including participation in sports teams, participation in individual sports, walking for exercise, workouts at gyms and participation in dance or exercise classes. It was found that the average number of hours spent in physical exercise activities since adolescence was a significant predictor of reduced breast-cancer risk. The data suggested that women who maintain an activity level of 1–3 hours per week could reduce their risk of premenopausal breast cancer by about 30 per cent and those who maintain an activity level of at least four hours per week might reduce their risk by more than 50 per cent.

(Exercise Psychology 1.1, Exercise and its relation to cancer)

Social approach

Social psychology is one of the dominant approaches in Sports and Exercise Psychology. There is a whole section of this option devoted to social-approach studies so there should be no shortage of material for you to cite if you have studied this option.

Carron, Bray and Eys (2002) examined the relationship between task cohesiveness and team success in sport. Nearly 300 Canadian competitive basketball and soccer players were asked to respond to a questionnaire about group cohesion. The results of the study provided evidence of a very strong relationship between cohesion and success in both sports. The results also showed that perceptions of team task cohesiveness were relatively consistent among members of the same team, suggesting that the measure used was a valid indicator of team cohesion. The researchers adopted stringent criteria for assessment of statistical significance and they also analysed results for consistency across individuals. This suggests that the results are reliable and that this study has provided valid insights into the role of group cohesion in sporting success.

(Social Psychology of Sport 1.3, Aspects of cohesion)

Individual-differences approach

Although all the individual-differences approach studies you came across at AS are devoted to psychological dysfunction it is important to recognise that the individual differences approach is much broader than that. Any research relating to personality or cognitive ability has a basis in individual differences. There are therefore a number of theories and studies in Sport and Exercise Psychology that can be cited with reference to this approach. Once again the title of one of the option sections, **Sport and the Individual,** is a guide to where you might look for examples such as Eysenck's and Cattell's personality theories.

Eysenck, Nias and Cox (1982) is a study in which Eysenck applied his personality theory to the sporting arena. He found that sports people tend to be high on extraversion and psychoticism and low on neuroticism. He explained these findings in terms of sports performers having low cortical arousal (typical of extraverts) leading to sensation-seeking, high psychoticism being associated with competitiveness/aggression and that high levels of anxiety would impede sporting performance.

(Sport and the Individual 1.3, Relevance of personality in sport)

Developmental approach

The developmental approach is not one that is central to Sports and Exercise Psychology. However, this is a gap in the research as many young people are involved in rigorous sport training and the pressures are considerable on young people in a wide range of sports. Also theories of exercise and mental/physical health are relevant to people throughout the lifespan.

Although not identified as a key study, one relevant study discussed in *OCR A2 Psychology* (p.263) that could be cited in terms of application to sport of the developmental approach is **Coakley (1992)**. This is a study on burnout in young athletes. Fifteen young sports performers were interviewed as a result of which the researcher identified the causes of burnout as lying in the organisation of high-performance sport. Young athletes frequently feel that they are not in control of their lives because they have to obey rigorous training schedules and inevitably have to make lifestyle 'choices' that prevent them from leading normal teenage lives. Coakley argued that for this reason changes should be made in the way that sporting commitments are integrated into the lives of young athletes and also that there should be changes in parent–child and coach–athlete dynamics that allow young people more control over their lives.

(Exercise Psychology 3.1, Burnout and withdrawal)

Behaviourist perspective

The behaviourist perspective is not fundamental to sports and exercise psychology but it is possible to find a few studies that are informed by behaviourism.

Berkowitz and Geen (1966) is a study that has similarities with Bandura *et al.* (1961) in that it involves cued aggression. It was a laboratory experiment in which the hypothesis that aggressive behaviour may be evoked by environmental cues was tested. The study was based on 88 male university students who were introduced to a stooge named either 'Kirk' or 'Bob' who either angered them or treated them in a neutral fashion. They then watched a film clip of a prize-fight in which the actor Kirk Douglas received a beating, or an exciting film clip of a track race. Participants were then allowed to deliver mild electric shocks to the stooge they had met. Berkowitz and Geen found that the highest numbers of shocks were administered by participants who had experienced anger arousal, watched the prize fight and to whom the stooge had been introduced as 'Kirk'. The simple name association heightened the stooge's cue value for aggressive responses from those who were ready to act aggressively. This study is based on classical conditioning (stimulus–response relationship).

(Sport and the Individual 2.2, Social theories)

Psychodynamic perspective

The psychodynamic perspective has limited relevance to Sport and Exercise Psychology. However, one theory of aggression has psychodynamic roots.

Although not identified as a key study, one theory discussed in *OCR A2 Psychology* (p.198) that can be cited in terms of application to sport of the psychodynamic perspective is Freud's catharsis theory. Freud considered aggression to be a basic human instinct, but one that followed from a more primary instinct, the death drive/instinct (later called *thanatos*). Freud believed that human behaviour is driven by the conflicting drive towards self-destruction and *eros,* the love or sex drive, the innate drive towards life. According to Freud *eros* displaces self-destructive energy and as a consequence negative feelings are redirected against others in the form of aggression. The release of pent-up aggression was termed *catharsis* by Freud. Some sports psychologists have argued that controlled aggression on the sports field is a valuable way of releasing pent-up aggression and hence enabling young men in particular to experience catharsis, thus distracting them from potentially more dangerous outlets for aggression.

(Sport and the Individual 2.1, Instinct theories)

5.5 Psychology of Education examples: approaches and perspectives

Cognitive approach

Given that learning is a cognitive process it will not come as a surprise to learn that the cognitive approach is one of the most important approaches in the Psychology of Education.

Klahr and Nigam (2004) undertook a study to compare the effects of direct instruction with discovery learning on children's mastery of an elementary-school science objective, a method for creating experiments. This was an independent-samples experiment involving 112 children aged 8–10 years. In the direct-instruction condition the children were taught how to carry out the experiment. In the discovery-learning condition the children were encouraged to try to work out how to conduct the experiment themselves through trial and error of their own designs without instruction or feedback. Significantly more children learned how to carry out the experiment through direct instruction than discovery learning. Moreover, the effects were carried over to a second stage of the study in which children were asked to critique a poster for a science fair. A higher number of valid critical points were made by those who had undergone direct teaching than discovery learning.

(Teaching and Learning 3.2, Cognitive approaches to learning)

Physiological approach

There are not many physiological studies included in the *OCR A2 Psychology of Education* syllabus. This is to be regretted as, increasingly, physiological-approach research such as studies based on brain-scanning technology are proving valuable in terms of understanding learning difficulties such as dyslexia. One part of the syllabus that does lend itself to physiological studies is the section on brain differences between males and females.

Kimura (2002) reviewed recent physiological studies of differences between male and female brains. She suggested that the effects of sex hormones on brain organisation occur so early in life that from the start gender differences are 'hard wired'. However, brain plasticity then results in brain structure being subject also to environmental effects that are hard to measure. Differential exposure to sex hormones may explain different levels of aggression and nurturing in men and women. Kimura suggests that the sex differences in intelligence reflect different types of ability rather than levels of ability. This explains the reliable findings that males are generally better at spatial/navigational tasks while females have superior language abilities.

(Enabling learning: dealing with diversity 3.2, Differences in brain structure)

Social approach

The social approach is increasingly seen as a key approach in the field of Psychology of Education. As with Sport and Exercise Psychology, a whole section of this applied option is devoted to social-approach studies and there are also a number of social-approach studies in other sections of the Psychology of Education option. You can cite here Vygotsky's theories as he focused on the social interactions of the child.

Ilatov et al. (1998) is a social-approach study that investigated whether teacher–student interactions are influenced by gender, teacher style and/or academic attainment of students. It was an observational study conducted in the classrooms of two teachers in a senior school in Israel. Data were collected by videotaping and analysing teacher–pupil interactions in class. It was found that the 'personality' of each class influenced the whole spectrum of teachers' behaviours. Important differences between the two classes were found in the gender-related patterns of both teachers' and students' classroom talk. Females dominated one class academically while the other was not dominated by either gender. Weaker students attracted more attention from one teacher and in one class they happened to be boys. However, personal characteristics and student–student relationships also played a role. Neither teacher showed any bias against females so the finding did not support previous studies that have indicated that males get more attention from teachers than females.

(The social world of teaching and learning 3.1, Comparison of student–teacher communications)

Individual-differences approach

There was a time when the individual-differences approach dominated the world of educational psychology. Most of the focus traditionally was on the individual child as a learner and individual differences in cognitive ability. However, this approach has become less central as emphasis has shifted towards the needs of groups rather than individuals, and individual progress has been seen in terms of the educational environment rather than individual differences between children.

Heller (2004) is an exception in this syllabus as it focuses on the needs of the individual child and in particular in the identification of individual differences in cognitive ability that require teacher adjustment in order to fully meet those needs. Heller argues that having a gifted child in your class does not necessarily mean that you have a child who will be easy to teach. In fact, Heller warns that behaviours typical of gifted children can be interpreted in different ways by teachers. While some may welcome the critical and demanding approach to learning that is often found in gifted children, other teachers may interpret behaviour such as frequent questioning an irritant and a problem. Although ability grouping in theory might be thought to facilitate the learning of gifted children, in fact even within a top set individual differences in ability can be very large, so teachers still need to employ different skills in order to engage the gifted child.

(Enabling learning: dealing with diversity 1.2, Provision for gifted and talented students)

Developmental approach

In one sense the whole of the Psychology of Education applied option is concerned with developmental psychology as it deals with the learning of children during the early stages of development. For theories that are explicitly development you can cite Piaget, Freud, Vygotsky, Bruner or Erikson!

You may well want to stick to Piaget or Samuel and Bryant for an educational application of the developmental approach but if you want to branch out you could introduce Erikson's eight-stage theory of development. **Erikson** described the primary school age as one of 'industry and inferiority'. This is a stage at which children are eager to work hard and please their teacher (industry). However if they suffer from bullying or low attainment they can suffer from low self-esteem (inferiority) and this can negatively impact on their attitude towards school and learning.

(The social world of teaching and learning 1.1, Developmental stages such as industry/inferiority)

Behaviourist perspective

As behaviourism is all about learning, one might expect to find quite a few behaviourist perspective studies in Psychology of Education. In fact, behaviourism is not represented by many studies in the OCR specification. Behaviourist approaches are used in schools mainly to encourage good behaviour (positive reinforcement) rather than being seen as key to children's learning (defined as knowledge acquisition). You can cite Skinner and his pigeons, but remember to link it in with children's behaviour and the use of reinforcement strategies like stickers and house points.

One study that applies the behaviourist perspective to learning (knowledge acquisition) is **Ausubel (1960).** This is a laboratory experiment devised to test the hypothesis that cognitive structure is hierarchically organised. This means that we categorise information in terms of highly inclusive concepts that subsume less inclusive subconcepts and informational data. Behaviourists assume both that this organisational structure holds true and that as we learn and acquire new knowledge those new data are incorporated into the existing cognitive structure if the new data are subsumable under relevant existing categories. Ausubel tested this hypothesis on 120 teacher-training students. The students were given an unfamiliar passage to learn. Some were helped by being prepared with an organiser passage while others were not. Ausubel found that there was a near significant difference in scores on a multiple-choice test administered afterwards with participants who had been given advance organisers scoring higher than those who had not. Ausubel concluded that advance organisers probably facilitate learning and retention of new material.

(Teaching and learning 3.1, Behaviourist use of objectives and monitoring of tasks)

Psychodynamic perspective

There are no studies from the psychodynamic perspective suggested in the OCR specification for the Psychology of Education option so you may need to refer back to Freud's stages of psychosexual development and Little Hans.

5.6 Debates in psychology

You need to know about several key debates in psychology and to be able to provide examples of what can be learned about these debates from psychological studies you have read for AS or in your study of the A2 applied options. You need to understand the debates and be able to apply your knowledge in the context of psychological research to answer part (e) of section B. No examples of studies have been given because most studies can be discussed from the perspective of several different debates. Guidance as to which debates and issues are central to particular studies can be found in *Psychology A2 for OCR* and the *OCR A2 Psychology Key Studies Companion*.

5.6.1 Determinism and free will

Determinism is the view that all behaviours and mental acts such as thoughts are determined by factors beyond our control.

A belief in free will is the belief that our behaviours and mental acts are the products of our own choice and will.

- Determinist explanations can be biological or environmental. Biological determinism explains behaviours in terms of biochemical factors such as hormones, genetic factors and physiological factors such as brain structure. Environmental determinism might explain behaviour in terms of factors such as upbringing, environment and experiences.

- A free-will explanation emphasises that humans have the cognitive ability to make choices about their actions.

5.6.2 Reductionism and holism

Reductionism is the process of breaking down phenomena into their constituent parts. This is a process that is seen as positive in sciences like chemistry, but in psychology it is often criticised for oversimplifying human behaviour.

Holism is an approach that attempts to take into account a whole range of factors that might together explain human behaviours.

5.6.3 The nature–nurture debate

This debate centres on whether behaviours are innate (inborn or genetically determined), i.e. the result of nature, or whether they are acquired as a result of experience or environmental influences (nurture). Both nature and nurture can be seen as determinist because they offer no scope for the role of free will.

5.6.4 Individual and situational explanations

Individual (dispositional) explanations locate the causes of behaviours in individual characteristics that may be innate or at least located in the individual's personality.

Situational explanations explain behaviours in terms of environmental factors such as family and neighbourhood or situational or circumstantial triggers such as events or the behaviours of others.

5.6.5 Ethnocentrism

The original meaning of ethnocentrism is a belief in the superiority of one's own group (ethnic group or culture). However, it is nowadays normally taken to mean not a belief in the superiority of one's own group but the inability to think outside one's own cultural experience and a tendency to assume that what happens in our own culture is common to other cultures. In research terms this means that psychologists sometime draw conclusions from the experience of their own culture or group and mistakenly assume it can be generalised to other groups or cultures.

5.6.6 Psychology as science

The issue of whether psychology is a science has long been the subject of debate.

Arguments for:

- Psychologists often use the scientific method of testing hypotheses by manipulation of IVs and rigorous control of procedures.

Arguments against:

- Psychologists study human behaviour and humans cannot be investigated in the same objective way as the physical materials or forces that are investigated in sciences such as chemistry and physics.
- Psychologists are to a large degree concerned with internal mental processes that are not directly observable and therefore not open to scientific scrutiny.

5.6.7 Usefulness of psychological research

This is classified by OCR as a debate but it is more properly an issue and is in fact applied to questions in the alternative section B question on research methods and issues. Usefulness of psychological research depends on both its practical applications and its intrinsic value. To have value research should be valid. To be valid, research should have face validity (it should do what it sets out to do), it should be high in ecological validity, it should abide by ethical guidelines and be generalisable.

5.7 Using your knowledge in Unit G544

In this section you will be given guidance on how to answer the approaches question of section B. We will take the cognitive approach as our example and the debates on whether psychology is a science and ethnocentrism.

5.7.1 Answering cognitive-approach questions

Part (a) specimen exam question

Q (a) Using your knowledge of psychology briefly outline the cognitive approach. (4 marks)

To answer part (a) of section B you will need to refer back to Chapter 1, which defines the approaches and outlines the assumption of each approach. You should refer to assumptions such as that it is possible to study mental processes scientifically and that the human mind can be viewed as an information processor somewhat analogous to a computer.

Part (b) specimen exam question

Q (b) Describe two pieces of research that use the cognitive approach. (8 marks)

To answer part (b) you need to learn and describe two pieces of research from the approach or perspective in question. You can use AS examples or A2 examples from the options you have studied such as those outlined above.

Part (c) specimen exam question

Q (c) Discuss the strengths and limitations of using the cognitive approach to explain behaviour. Use examples of psychological research to support your answer. (12 marks)

To answer this question you need 1) to identify general strengths and limitations of cognitive-approach studies, then 2) to explain these using supporting evidence from either AS Core Studies or A2 option key studies.

- Strengths of the cognitive approach are the application of the scientific method, control of variables and, if the experimental method is used, the possibility of determining cause and effect.

- Weaknesses of the cognitive approach is that experiments tend to lack ecological validity and that they frequently rely on self-report as internal cognitive processes cannot be investigated by direct observation.

Here is a likely answer to the above question based on a mixture of AS and A2 studies.

A (c) One strength of the cognitive approach is that it often uses the experimental approach, which allows variables to be controlled and cause and effect to be identified. For example, in Loftus and Palmer all the participants watched the same video clips and then answered the same questionnaire. Only the IV (the verb in the critical question) was different in the two conditions, which allowed its effect to be measured. This experiment showed that recall of an incident can be affected by questions asked afterwards, showing the police that they should be very cautious in their approach to examining eyewitnesses in case they distort people's memories. In Loftus, Loftus and Messo, all the participants watched the same series of slides of an incident in a fast food outlet, then afterwards answered the same questionnaire and were given the same 12 faces to identify the person in the incident. The only variable that was altered was the IV. In one condition the person to be identified merely paid a cheque, in the other he drew a gun. The results showed that the presence of the gun distracted attention from the person in the scene and other details, with the result that participants in the weapon condition did not recall as much detail as the other participants and were not as successful in identifying the person involved. This shows that people's memory for events and their ability to identify suspects is variable and dependent on the context of the event.

One weakness of the cognitive approach is that it often relies on self-report for data as internal mental processes cannot be directly observed. This means that objective data cannot be collected. For example, in Zalewska-Puchala *et al.* over 100 nurses completed self-report measures of self-efficacy and their engagement in health behaviours. However, this study did not actually measure participants' engagement in health behaviours but relied on them reporting how much they smoke, drank, took exercise, etc. This casts doubt on the findings as the measure may not be reliable as people may not tell the truth about their behaviour. Another weakness of the cognitive approach is that it often uses experiments that are low in ecological validity. For example, in both Loftus and Palmer and Loftus, Loftus and Messo the participants were all undergraduate students and the materials used were video clips of car crashes and slides of a dramatic enactment of a crime. Watching these visual aids would be a completely different experience from being an eyewitness to a real-life crime (because of arousal, emotion, etc.) so these studies are low in ecological validity, which reduces the validity and generalisability of their findings.

Part (d) specimen exam question

Q (d) Compare the cognitive approach to the behaviourist perspective. Use examples of psychological research to support your answer. (8 marks)

To answer part (d) questions you need to understand and explain using supporting evidence the similarities and differences between the approach in question and any other approach or perspective.

This is an example of a question that is easier to answer well if you are able to cite some A2 studies rather than just AS Core Studies.

NB: the term 'compare' invites you to comment on similarities and differences. In order to answer this question you need to identify and explain using supporting evidence at least two similarities or two differences or one similarity and one difference.

- Similarities include adoption of the scientific method, control of variables, focus on learning as key to behaviour.

- Differences include the fact that behaviourists focus on observable behaviours whereas cognitive psychologists are more interested in internal mental processes that are not observable.

Here is a likely answer to part d) based on AS and A2 studies.

A (d) The cognitive and behavioural approaches share a commitment to the scientific method. This means that they test hypotheses, often use laboratory experiments and control variables. One example of the behaviourist approach is Bandura's study of imitation of aggression in children. Bandura recognised that operant-conditioning studies on animals did not really apply to humans because of their cognitive ability. He therefore developed social-learning theory, which brought together behaviourism and cognition. Bandura hypothesised that children would learn to imitate aggression through watching an adult engage in aggressive acts. He conducted a well-controlled experiment in which children were all put through a standardised procedure with the only difference being whether they observed an aggressive model, a non-aggressive model or no model. The DV was imitation of aggressive acts and, as it was a behaviourist study, observation was the method used to measure the DV. A cognitive example that shares the scientific, experimental approach is Klahr and Nigam, who also conducted an experiment using children. They wanted to test whether children learned how to conduct a simple scientific study better through direct teaching or discovery learning. Like Bandura they controlled variables and manipulated the IV (mode of learning). They found that children who were directly taught learned better than those who were exposed to learning through trial and error. They also used observation to find out what the children had learned but they also tested them using a self-report method (interview). A difference between the behavioural and cognitive approaches is that behaviourists theorise that all learning is environmental, which is reductionist, whereas cognitive psychologists tend to take a more holistic view and believe that learning is the outcome of physiology as well as experience. Bandura et al. focused on the imitation of aggressive acts but did not discuss in detail the differences found between male and female children that could be innate. Bandura did, however, match children on observed levels of aggressive behaviour before the start of the study. Klahr and Nigam found that some children did not need teaching as they already understood how to control variables in a scientific experiment and the data from these children were removed from the study as Klahr and Nigam wanted to focus specifically on the effects of different teaching methods.

Part (e) specimen exam question

Q (e) Discuss aspects of the cognitive approach that support the argument that psychology is a science. (8 marks)

To answer part (e) questions you need to be able to apply your understanding of the approaches and perspectives and your knowledge of the studies in relation to a debate. One of the key debates regarding psychology is whether it is a science or not (see above, p.130). This part of section B is asking you to consider the same issues that we have discussed in responding to parts (a)-(d), namely the way in which the cognitive approach uses the scientific method – hypothesis testing, IV and DV, control of variables, etc. However, you should also consider evidence that cognitive research is not as scientific as its exponents would like it to be. That is because cognitive–approach studies tend to deal with internal mental processes that are not directly observable and hence difficult to study scientifically.

Here is an alternative part (e) question.

Q (e) Using your knowledge of psychology discuss the extent to which cognitive-approach studies are ethnocentric.

This question requires you to provide examples of cognitive research and discuss the degree to which they show ethnocentrism. Ethnocentrism may be interpreted as being culture-blind or focusing on one's own group. Cognitive studies are often conducted in universities and frequently use students as participants. This limits generalisability of the research as conclusions tend to be drawn on the basis of a sample that is not representative of either the wider population in the students' own country or the wider international community. Sometimes researchers report the ethnic mix in their sample but this is quite rare. You may discuss AS examples, e.g. Loftus and Palmer, or any of the many cognitive studies covered in the A2 options. Many cognitive studies reported are conducted in US colleges or UK universities, but in the OCR A2 Psychology textbook some studies from other European countries or even occasionally from other areas of the world such as the Far East are cited. Just because such studies are not from the US or the UK does not mean they are not ethnocentric! However, if European or Asian researchers apply measures standardised in the US, for example, this shows that they are not ethnocentric in terms of being focused only on their own culture but are keen for their research to contribute to cross-cultural understanding.

5.7.2 Answering physiological-approach questions

You should be able to apply the strategy explained above to answer questions on any approach or section. For the remaining sections you will be offered guidance rather than specimen answers.

Q (a) Using your knowledge of psychology briefly outline the physiological approach. (4 marks)

Refer back to Chapter 1, p.5 to help you answer this question. Likely answers will refer to assumptions, e.g. that there are genetic patterns of behaviour and physiological correlates of behaviour, and to the use of technology such as brain scans to investigate those physiological correlates.

Q (b) Describe two pieces of research that use the physiological approach. (8 marks)

In answering this question you may refer to physiological approach Core Studies and/or to physiological studies you have met at A2.

Q (c) Discuss the strengths and limitations of using the physiological approach to explain behaviour. Use examples of psychological research to support your answer. (12 marks)

To answer this question you need 1) to identify general strengths and limitations of physiological-approach studies, then 2) to explain these using supporting evidence from either AS Core Studies or A2 option key studies.

● Strengths of the physiological approach are the use of technology to produce objective data regarding physiological correlates of behaviours, and the rigorous application of the scientific method including careful control of participant variables.

● A weakness of the physiological approach is that much empirical research is correlational and therefore cause and effect cannot be determined.

Q (d) Compare the physiological approach to the cognitive approach. Use examples of psychological research to support your answer. (8 marks)

In order to answer this question you need to identify and support with evidence at least one similarity and one difference or two similarities or differences.

● Similarities include adoption of the scientific method and control of variables.

● Differences include the fact that physiological-approach psychologists focus on investigating physiological correlates of mental processes and behaviour whereas cognitive psychologists usually analyse behaviour for evidence of behaviour. Another difference is that physiological research is generally correlational while cognitive psychologists tend to use the experimental method.

Q (e) Discuss how the physiological approach can help our understanding of human behaviour. (8 marks)

This is an example of a question that will probably be much better answered if you are able to cite some A2 studies rather than just AS Core Studies. Although Dement and Kleitman, Sperry and

Maguire are interesting studies they have less direct relevance to this question than some of the valuable physiological studies discussed at A2, e.g. Raine *et al.*, Caspi *et al.* (Forensic); a number of studies in health and clinical on the physiological/genetic origins of disorders such as schizophrenia, depression and eating disorders (e.g. Kendler *et al.*); studies on the physiological benefits of exercise (e.g. Bernstein *et al.*) or brain differences between men and women (Kimura). Although no specific debate is referred to in this question, a high-level answer might consider some of the debates in evaluating physiological-approach research, e.g. reductionism/holism, nature/nurture, etc.

5.7.3 Answering social-approach questions

Q (a) Using your knowledge of psychology briefly outline the social approach. (4 marks)

Refer back to Chapter 1, p.8 to help you answer this question. Likely answers will refer to assumptions of the social approach such as that human behaviour is best understood in a social context and that social psychologists focus on social interactions, group dynamics, etc.

Q (b) Describe two pieces of research that use the social approach. (8 marks)

In answering this question you may refer to social-approach Core Studies and/or to social studies you have met at A2.

Q (c) Discuss the strengths and limitations of using the social approach to explain behaviour. Use examples of social research to support your answer. (12 marks)

To answer this question you need 1) to identify general strengths and limitations of social-approach studies, then 2) to explain these using supporting evidence from either AS Core Studies or A2 option key studies.

- Strengths of the social approach are that social-approach studies raise important issues like obedience and conformity; they broaden our understanding of human behaviour by moving the focus from the individual to human interactions; application of scientific method – use of experiments to determine cause and effect; wide range of methods used including self-report; observation and collection of both quantitative and qualitative data.

- A weakness of the social approach is that it is hard to control participant variables when the subject of study is human interaction. Another weakness of the social approach is that social-approach experimental studies are particularly lacking in ecological validity for the same reason – human interactions are difficult to control and the more you control them the less like real life they become.

Q (d) Compare the social approach to the physiological approach. Use examples of psychological research to support your answer. (8 marks)

In order to answer this question you need to identify and support with evidence at least one similarity and one difference or two similarities or differences.

- Similarities include adoption of the scientific method.

- Differences include the fact that social psychologists focus on human interactions and the effects of environment on human behaviour while the physiological approach takes an individual approach and focuses on innate characteristics. Another difference is that social psychologists use a wide variety of methods and undertake both qualitative and quantitative research while physiological research is generally quantitative and correlational.

Q (e) Discuss how the social approach can inform our understanding of how situational factors affect human behaviour. (8 marks)

In responding to this question it is important to focus on what is unique in terms of what the social approach contributes to our understanding of the individual/situational debate. For example, Milgram explores the effects of situation (the conduct of his experiment in a prestigious university and the presence of a scientist in a grey coat) on people's willingness to obey orders against their moral code. Another study to cite here is Wikström's study of youth offending, which shows the importance of peer pressure in encouraging offending behaviour. Much youth offending occurs in the presence of others. Vygotsky's work on the role of environment in children's learning could also be mentioned in support of situational factors. On the other side of the argument you could argue that social psychology does not really focus on individual factors that are also important in shaping human behaviour.

5.7.4 Answering individual-differences approach questions

Q (a) Using your knowledge of psychology briefly outline the individual-differences approach. (4 marks)

Refer back to Chapter 1, p.10 to help you answer this question. Likely answers will refer to the assumption that humans are unique individuals and that it is as important to understand the differences between individuals as to understand the general rules of human behaviour.

Q (b) Describe two pieces of research that use the individual-differences approach. (8 marks)

In answering this question you may describe individual-differences approach Core Studies and/or individual-differences approach studies you have met at A2.

Q (c) Discuss the strengths and limitations of using the individual-differences approach to explain behaviour. Use examples of research to support your answer. (12 marks)

To answer this question you need 1) to identify general strengths and limitations of individual-differences approach studies, then 2) to explain these using supporting evidence from either AS Core Studies or A2 option key studies.

- Strengths of the individual-differences approach is that it enable us to better understand the whole spectrum of human behaviour. Whereas most psychological research focuses on average behaviours, the individual-difference approach helps us understand how and why some individuals differ from 'the norm'.

- A weakness of the individual-differences approach is that it is hard to make predictions about human behaviour on the basis of the studies.

Q (d) Compare the individual-differences approach to the developmental approach. Use examples of psychological research to support your answer. (8 marks)

In order to answer this question you need to identify and support with evidence at least one similarity and one difference or two similarities or differences.

- A similarity between the developmental approach and the individual-differences approach is that neither is associated with one research method over another. Researchers from both approaches will use a variety of methods such as cognitive tests, self-report and experiments to explain human behaviour.

- Differences include the fact that developmental psychologists tend to work in terms of universal stages of development and age norms whereas individual differences psychologists focus on what makes one individual different from another.

Q (e) Discuss how the individual–differences approach can inform our understanding of the nature–nurture debate. (8 marks)

In responding to this question it is important to focus on the nature–nurture debate (see above, p.129). The AS Core Studies illustrate how individuals may differ in psychological health (e.g. Griffiths on gambling addiction) but they do not show whether this is down to nature or nurture. Individual-difference studies in sport show that personality variables matter in terms of sporting achievement and motivation. Reliable measures (such as Eysenck and Cattell) show that these are stable factors and not much affected by experiences so they are probably down to nature rather than nurture. Forensic psychology also shows that while there are situational differences that contribute to offending behaviours there are also individual differences in personality (risk-taking personalities) that contribute to risk of offending (Wikström; Palmer and Hollin) and that these are again stable therefore probably due to nature rather than nurture.

5.7.5 Answering developmental-approach questions

Q (a) Using your knowledge of psychology briefly outline the developmental approach. (4 marks)

Refer back to Chapter 1, p.11 to help you answer this question. Likely answers will refer to the assumption that development occurs over the lifetime and that development through predetermined stages is universal.

Q (b) Describe two pieces of research that use the developmental approach. (8 marks)

In answering this question you may describe developmental approach Core Studies and/or developmental-approach studies you have met at A2.

Q (c) Discuss the strengths and limitations of using the development approach to explain human behaviour. Use examples of research to support your answer. (12 marks)

To answer this question you need 1) to identify general strengths and limitations of developmental-approach studies, then 2) to explain these using supporting evidence from either AS Core Studies or A2 option key studies.

- Strengths of the developmental approach is that it enables us to better understand how change occurs over the lifespan. Much developmental research is longitudinal so it can provide rich data over time. Another strength is that it uses a wide variety of research methods such as experiments, self-report and observations in exploring human development.

- A weakness of the developmental approach is that research can raise ethical issues as it often uses children as participants.

Q (d) Compare the developmental approach to the cognitive approach. Use examples of psychological research to support your answer. (8 marks)

In order to answer this question you need to identify and support with evidence at least one similarity and one difference or two similarities or differences.

- A similarity between them is that they both often use the experimental method.

Another similarity is that they both focus to a large extent on cognitive processes such as learning and language.

- One difference between them is that developmental psychologists are also interested in interactions between people such as teacher–child interactions while cognitive psychologists focus on internal processes.

Q (e) Discuss what the developmental approach contributes to the determinism/free will debate. (8 marks)

In responding to this question it is important to focus on the determinism/free will debate rather than summarising developmental studies (see below, p.129). The AS developmental Core Studies probably weigh on the determinist side – Samuel and Bryant follow Piaget's determinist stages of development; Freud – also determinist: children follow stages of psychosocial development; and Bandura – determinist in that children who see aggression will imitate that aggression (i.e. without exercising free will). Forensic-psychology developmental studies are also fairly determinist – Juby and Farrington discuss the effects of factors such as criminal parents and disrupted families on children turning to crime. Similarly, Wikström identifies individual and situational factors that increase risk of crime. But are they really determinist? Both Farrington and Wikström acknowledge that there is no straightforward link between poverty and crime or disrupted families and crime. Many youngsters who grow up in deprived neighbourhoods are honest and others who are brought up in an affluent home are not. Does this lend support for free will? Or are we genetically determined to be honest or dishonest?

5.7.6 Answering behaviourist-perspective questions

Q (a) Using your knowledge of psychology briefly outline the behaviourist perspective. (4 marks)

Refer back to Chapter 1, p.13 to help you answer this question. Likely answers will refer to the behaviourist assumption that all learning is the result of the stimulus–response relationship and that while animals learn through operant conditioning people can also learn through imitation (social learning theory).

Q (b) Describe two pieces of research from the behaviourist perspective. (8 marks)

This may well be difficult to do if you only rely on AS material. The only AS Core Study that is behaviourist is Bandura *et al*. You should therefore be prepared to use behaviourist studies used in the applied options to answer this fully.

Q (c) Discuss the strengths and limitations of using the behaviourist perspective to explain human behaviour. Use examples of research to support your answer. (12 marks)

To answer this question you need 1) to identify general strengths and limitations of behaviourist perspective studies, then 2) to explain these using supporting evidence from either AS Core Studies or A2 option key studies.

- Strengths of the behaviourist perspective are that it was the first attempt to study human behaviour scientifically. Another strength is that it has proved useful in explaining and treating a wide range of psychological disorders.

- A weakness of the behaviourist perspective is that it is reductionist. It fails to take sufficient account of the role of either free will in human behaviour or of innate physiological factors that shape behaviour.

Q (d) Compare the behaviourist perspective to the individual-differences approach. Use examples of psychological research to support your answer. (8 marks)

In order to answer this question you need to identify and support with evidence at least one similarity and one difference or two similarities or differences.

● A similarity between them is that they are both reductionist in that behaviourism reduces human behaviour to environmental factors while individual-differences approach psychologists tend to reduce behaviour to innate individual differences.

● One difference between them is that behaviourist psychologists are interested in applying general rules of human behaviour while individual-differences psychologists are interested in what makes individuals unique.

Q (e) Discuss how behaviourist perspective theories/studies relate to the reductionist/holist debate. (8 marks)

In responding to this question it is important to explain what is meant by reductionism and holism and then to discuss the extent to which examples of behaviourist perspective theories and studies are reductionist or holist (see above, p.129). This can be discussed by reference to the originators of conditioning theories e.g. Pavlov and Skinner. However account should also be taken of more sophisticated applications of behaviourist theory such as Bandura (Social Learning Theory and self-efficacy); Seligman and Lewinsohn (learned helplessness and learned hopelessness). Reference could also be made to the fact that cognitive-behavioural therapies, while they may be reductionist, have been found very useful in the treatment of psychological disorders.

5.7.7 Answering psychodynamic-perspective questions

Q (a) Using your knowledge of psychology, briefly outline the psychodynamic perspective. (4 marks)

Refer back to Chapter 1, p.15 to help you answer this question. Likely answers will refer to the assumption that psychodynamic theory suggests that all human actions are the result of unconscious desires, drives and fears and that human behaviour is shaped by internal rather than external factors.

Q (b) Describe two pieces of research that use the psychodynamic perspective. (8 marks)

In answering this question it would probably be safest to stick with the AS studies (Freud and Thigpen and Cleckley) as there are not really any good examples of psychodynamic perspective research in the A2 applied options.

Q (c) Discuss the strengths and limitations of using the psychodynamic approach to explain human behaviour. Use examples of research to support your answer. (12 marks)

To answer this question you need 1) to identify general strengths and limitations of psychodynamic theories, then 2) to explain these using supporting evidence from the AS Core Studies or A2 option key theories/studies if you have come across any.

● A strength of the psychodynamic approach is that it brought into the remit of psychology the role of the subconscious and behaviours that cannot be observed such as dreaming.

● A weakness of the psychodynamic approach is that it is based on theory that cannot be supported through scientific study.

Q (d) Compare the psychodynamic approach to the social approach. Use examples of psychological research to support your answer. (8 marks)

In order to answer this question you need to identify and support with evidence at least one similarity and one difference or two similarities or differences.

- It is not easy to find similarities between social-approach studies and psychodynamic theories and studies as they are very different.

- One difference between them is that psychodynamic perspective psychologists focus on the subconscious and behaviours that are not observable such as dreams while social psychologists focus on human interactions that are largely observable.

- Another difference is that social psychologists usually apply the scientific method while psychodynamic psychologists do not believe it necessary to study human behaviour scientifically.

Q (e) How does psychodynamic-perspective research relate to the debate about whether psychology is a science? (8 marks)

See above, p.130 for more on this debate.

Freud argued that because he dealt with individuals and the subconscious there was no need to apply the rules of the scientific method to his work. Psychodynamic research is therefore to weigh on the 'psychology is not a science' side of this debate. However, it is not necessary to reject on this basis the claim that psychology is a science. Instead, one could regard the psychodynamic approach as being separate from mainstream academic psychology.

As explained in the introduction to the previous chapter, in section B of G544 you have a choice of two questions. One is focused on approaches and perspectives (see previous chapter) while the other is focused on research methods and issues. See Table 6.1 for a list of the research methods and methodological issues that you will need to know. These are covered in sufficient detail in Chapter 2 (Data collection methods) and Chapter 3 (Issues in psychological investigations). In this chapter we will discuss how to use your knowledge and understanding to answer section B of G544.

6.1 Format of section B (Research Methods and Issues)   141

6.2 Examples of the experimental method (laboratory and field)   142

6.3 Examples of the observational method   144

6.4 Examples of the self-report method   144

6.5 Examples of the correlational method   145

6.6 Case-study method   146

6.7 Using your knowledge in Unit G544: Answering research methods and issues questions   148

Table 6.1 Research methods and issues

Research methods
Laboratory experiment
Field experiment
Observation
Self-report
Correlation
Case Study

Issues
Ecological validity
Ethics
Reliability and validity
Snapshot and longitudinal
Qualitative and quantitative
Usefulness

6.1 Format of section B (Research Methods and Issues)

This section of the exam usually follows a standard format. You are required to answer one five-part question. Parts (a)–(e) are worth 40 marks in total and all parts of this question are compulsory (with no choices) if you choose to answer it. The five parts will all relate primarily to one research method and one issue, although you will be asked to compare with a second research method and possibly to discuss a second methodological issue. Parts (a)–(b) require factual knowledge only while parts (c)–(e) require you to make evaluative points. Part (d) may ask you to compare two different research methods. Part (e) will link with an issue.

Here are examples based on the experimental research method and the issue of ecological validity:

Q (a) Using your knowledge of psychology briefly outline what is meant by ecological. (4 marks)
Q (b) Describe examples of high ecological validity from any <u>two</u> pieces of psychological research. (8 marks)
Q (c) Discuss the strengths and limitations of conducting psychological research where ecological validity is low. Use examples of psychological research to support your answer. (12 marks)
Q (d) Compare the ecological validity of laboratory experiments with the ecological validity of field experiments. Use examples of psychological research to support your answer. (8 marks)
Q (e) Discuss the usefulness of field experiments in psychology. (8 marks)

You may use AS studies only if you wish to in answering Section B questions but the examiners would prefer you to show knowledge of A2 studies as well and you will definitely be in a better position to answer some questions if you can draw on your A2 knowledge as well as the AS Core Studies. Before going on to give guidance on how to answer the questions we will turn first to A2 studies from each of the applied options that you might find useful for this section. The examples given here are studies selected as key studies in the accompanying textbook *Psychology A2 for OCR*. These are indicative of the studies you might wish to refer to. You should not feel restricted in any way to the examples shown here.

For information on which AS studies use the experimental method, turn to Chapter 2, p.21.

6.2 Examples of the experimental method (laboratory and field)

Examples from Forensic Psychology

There are many examples of laboratory experiments in Forensic Psychology, e.g. **Loftus, Loftus and Messo (1987)**. See Chapter 5, p.119 for summary.

Farrington, *et al.* **(2002)** is a **field experiment** in which two intensive regimes for young offenders based on behaviourist methods were investigated. This was an independent-measures experiment using an opportunity sample of young male offenders who were screened for suitability for open conditions and for the physical demands of an intervention regime. Each intervention group was compared with a control group of young offenders with a similar profile who were not selected for any intervention but left to serve their sentence in custody. Both regimes were physically demanding. One (Thorn Cross) was based on classroom skills; vocational training; life and social skills training and a community-release work placement. The other (Colchester) was run and staffed by Army personnel as well as prison personnel. It was based on drilling and physical training and consisted of three stages, which became gradually less restrictive. A common core of psychological tests was used to assess the impact of the intervention of participants' attitudes and behaviour. The percentage of offenders who were reconvicted following the skills-based programme was similar to the predicted percentage but the average time between release and reoffending was significantly longer for the intervention group than the control group. Moreover, the intervention participants cost society approximately £2,500 less than control offenders. During the two-year follow-up period participants who had undergone the military-style intervention committed slightly fewer offences on average than those in the control group. However, the average cost to society per person was very slightly higher for those in the experimental group than the control group because the crimes they committed were more serious.

Examples from Health and Clinical Psychology

There are several examples of laboratory experiments in Health and Clinical Psychology.

Ruiter *et al.* **(2001)** was an independent-measures experiment which examined the effect of fear arousal on attitude towards participating in self-examination for breast cancer. Eighty-eight female undergraduate students were randomly assigned to experimental conditions involving manipulation of fear level and strength of warning message. Participants were told that they would evaluate the effectiveness of several educational messages about breast cancer. These contained manipulation of fear. This was followed by a self-report measure of fear arousal. Next, participants read a persuasive message about performing monthly breast self-examination, supported by weak or strong arguments. Finally, a questionnaire was administered with post-experimental attitude towards breast self-examination as the DV. The main effect of manipulated fear was not statistically significant but there was a significant main effect of argument strength. There was also a significant interaction between reported fear and argument strength. Participants who expressed low fear did not differ in their attitude towards breast self-examination after reading either the weak or strong persuasive message whereas participants who reported mild fear indicated they were more positive towards breast self-examination after reading the strong persuasive message than the weak message.

Johansson and Aronsson (1984) was an independent measures **field experiment** on the effect of working with VDUs on stress at work. Participants were workers at a Swedish firm that was an early user of computers in the workplace. Workers responded to a questionnaire about their daily use of VDUs and other measures about work and stress and were divided into four groups on the basis of extent of VDU use. The four groups were compared in terms of general attitude to work, attitude to computerisation, mental strain and well-being. A second stage in the experiment involved taking regular physiological measures of stress from volunteers from both the low-VDU contact group and the high-VDU contact. The study found that those who worked extensively with VDUs showed more persistent effects of stress (adrenaline excretion) in the evenings after work.

Example from Sport and Exercise Psychology

There are several examples of laboratory experiments in Sport and Exercise Psychology e.g. **Berkowitz and Geen (1966).** See Chapter 5, p.125 for summary.

Brunelle, Janelle and Tennant (1999) is a **field experiment** in which the researchers studied the effect of cognitive/behavioural interventions in anger management among male soccer players. There were 57 male volunteer soccer players studying at an American university. Participants were randomly assigned to one of three treatment groups (anger awareness/role-playing/control group). Participants responded to self-report measures of anger, and angry behaviour was observed/measured during a fifteen-game round-robin season of competitive soccer games. Participants were told that the observation was focused on skill. Two dependent variables, angry behaviour and state anger, were analysed separately. Both dependent measures were calculated by averaging anger scores in the games played during pre-treatment, treatment and retention phases of the study. The researchers found that the role-playing and anger-awareness groups both displayed less angry behaviour than the control group during the treatment phase. During the retention phase the role-playing group showed less angry behaviour than the anger-awareness group and both experimental groups showed less angry behaviour than the control group.

Example from Psychology of Education

There are not many examples of laboratory experiments in Psychology of Education.

One example is **Ausubel (1960)**. See Chapter 5, p.128 for summary.

Burroughs-Lange (2008) was a longitudinal **field experiment** conducted to assess the effects of a reading intervention (Reading Recovery) on literacy progress in low-achieving children. This study followed up the impact on children's literacy in London schools a year or more after intervention had been received. In the 2005–6 school-year literacy progress was compared of the lowest achieving children in 42 schools serving disadvantaged urban areas. The researcher was not involved in the interventions. Progress of children on Reading Recovery was compared against progress of similar children in other schools who received other forms of intervention during the same period. In the year of the main study (2005–6), those children who received Reading Recovery achieved significant gains in all assessments compared with those who did not. In July 2007 the literacy achievement was again compared of those same children remaining in the same 42 schools. At the end of Year 2 the children who had received Reading Recovery in Year 1 were achieving within or above their chronological age band on all measures and were still around a year ahead of the comparison children in schools where Reading Recovery was not available. Moreover, the children who had taken Reading recovery showed progress in other aspects of the curriculum.

6.3 Examples of the observational method

Example from Forensic Psychology

One example of an observational study from Forensic Psychology is **Haney, Banks and Zimbardo (1973)**.

Example from Health and Clinical Psychology

One example of an observational study from Health and Clinical Psychology is **Lewinsohn *et al*. (1980)**. See Chapter 5, p.122 for summary.

Example from Sport and Exercise Psychology

One example of an observational study from Sport and Exercise Psychology is **Brunelle, Janelle and Tennant (1999)**. See above, p.143 for summary.

Example from Psychology of Education

One example of an observational study from Psychology of Education is **Ilatov *et al*. (1998)**. See Chapter 5, p.127 for summary.

6.4 Examples of the self-report method

Example from Forensic Psychology

One example of a self-report study from Forensic Psychology is **Akers *et al*. (1979)**. See Chapter 5, p.121 for summary.

Example from Health and Clinical Psychology

One example of a self-report study from Health and Clinical Psychology is **Zalewska–Puchala** *et al.* (2007). See Chapter 5, p.121 for summary.

Example from Sport and Exercise Psychology

One example of a self-report study from Sport and Exercise Psychology is **Carron, Bray and Eys (2002)**. See Chapter 5, p.124 for summary.

Example from Psychology of Education

Au, Watkins and Hattie (2010) is a longitudinal self-report study of the relationship between academic achievement and learned hopelessness in a sample of 741 secondary school students in Hong Kong. The researchers investigated correlations between affective–motivational characteristics of students such as prior academic failures, academic attributional style, self-efficacy, thoughts about intelligence, school values, learned hopelessness, self-esteem, learning strategy effectiveness and academic achievement. The participants completed a series of scales over a school year. As expected, prior achievement was the best predictor of subsequent achievement. The next best predictors were perceived learning difficulties and learned hopelessness. This in turn led to disengagement from schooling and students feeling responsible for their failures.

6.5 Examples of the correlational method

Example from Forensic Psychology

Gudjonsson and Sigurdsson (2007). Gudjonsson tested the validity of the Offending Motivation Questionnaire by correlating it with a range of other psychological measures on a sample of 128 male youths, age range 15-21, from Reykjavik, Iceland, who had been given a conditional discharge after a guilty plea. Most of the offences were property offences followed by car crimes, assault and criminal damage. The study showed that a compliant disposition is significantly related to participants' claim that they had been led or pressured into crime, or that they had been trying to please or impress peers by committing the offence. Perceived peer pressure can encourage youngsters to offend (e.g. doing a peer a favour, trying to impress, offending to earn a reputation, modelling other peers, and being unable to resist offending when encouraged or pressured to do so by peers). In this study excitement was the single most important motive given for the youths' offending (relating perhaps to findings by Farringdon *et al.* (2009) with regard to risk-taking disposition). The study also demonstrated the importance of anger in relation to the motivation for offending.

Example from Health and Clinical Psychology

One example of a correlational study from Health and Clinical Psychology is **Zalewska–Puchala** *et al.* (2007). See Chapter 5, p.121 for summary.

Example from Sport and Exercise Psychology

One example of a correlational study from Sport and Exercise Psychology is **Carron, Bray and Eys (2002)**. See Chapter 5, p.124 for summary.

Example from Psychology of Education

One example of a correlational study from Psychology of Education is **Au, Watkins and Hattie (2010)**. See above, p.145 for summary.

6.6 Case-study method

This is an additional method you need to know about for A2. It is not really new as several of the AS studies are case studies and you have probably already realised that they are investigations carried out in depth with small numbers of participants in order to collect rich data. They are often longitudinal in design. As is the case with correlations, they are not a method of data collection but rely on other methods (quasi-experiment, observation or self-report) for data collection.

6.6.1 Case studies in the AS Core Studies

Table 6.2 Case studies in the AS Core Studies

Case studies	Details
Savage-Rumbaugh	This can be classified as a longitudinal case study (two participants – Kanzi and Mulika). Data-collection method is observation.
Freud	This is a longitudinal case study of one boy's development (Little Hans) as observed and analysed by his father and Freud.
Dement and Kleitman	This can be described as a quasi experiment or a case study. Only five participants were studied in depth. Data-collection method was self-report and via EEG.
Sperry	This is a case study of eleven patients who had undergone hemisphere disconnection in order to explore the consequences of the surgery and hence localisation and lateralisation of brain function. Data-collection method is observation.
Reicher and Haslam	This is described by the researchers as a field experiment but it can also be described as a case study as there are 10 participants who are studied in depth over several days. Data-collection method is observation.
Rosenhan	Rosenhan's study 1 is a case study because it involved eight participants who self-referred to 12 hospitals in order to test diagnosis and treatment of psychological disorders. The pseudopatients collected data via participant observation.
Thigpen and Cleckley	This is a clinical case study of one patient who self-referred and was subsequently diagnosed with Multiple Personality Disorder. Data collection was via clinical interview.

6.6.2 A2 examples of case studies

Example from Forensic Psychology

Gudjonsson and MacKeith (1990) reported a case study of a 17-year-old youth who falsely confessed to two murders during police interrogation without a lawyer present, then confessed again during a second interview in the presence of a duty solicitor, and later made further misleading admissions to prison staff and another inmate while at the beginning of his remand. The confession appeared very detailed and apparently convincing but completely by chance the confession was subsequently proved to have been false. It appears to have resulted from persistent pressure and psychological manipulation of a young man who was at the time distressed and susceptible to the pressure of the interrogation. The youth was of average intelligence, suffered from no mental illness and his personality was not obviously abnormal. Charges were withdrawn and someone else was convicted of the offence.

Example from Health and Clinical Psychology

Budzynski et al. (1970) investigated the effect of a behavioural stress-management technique on patients who experienced moderate to severe recurring tension headaches. The technique they developed, the 'biofeedback' technique, was initially tested on individual patients as a series of case studies. The basic function of the 'biofeedback' instrumentation was to assist patients in reaching deep levels of muscle relaxation by means of analogue information feedback. Patients were trained to voluntarily lower their striate muscle tension in the face of daily life stresses and to reduce the incidence of tension headaches. Patients were instructed to practise relaxation techniques at home and they learned to carry over the technique shaped by the feedback tone to relaxing in silence. The muscle relaxation response described in this study suggests that operant conditioning techniques might be successfully applied to help with other physiological problems as well as to shape behaviours. Although Budzynski et al.'s pilot study appeared to lead to progress in patients controlling their stress symptoms, it could not provide objective data on the specific benefits of biofeedback because there was no control group.

Example from Sport and Exercise Psychology

Lacey (1950) is a case study which first challenged the undifferentiated approach to arousal. Twelve pregnant women were studied. They were required to undertake a difficult cognitive task while in a relaxed state. They were asked to wait for one minute before naming, as quickly as possible, all the words they could think of that began with a given letter for a period of three minutes. While they were undertaking this task measurements were made of diastolic and systolic blood pressure, palm conductance and heart rate. All individuals showed an increase in both systolic and diastolic blood pressure. Most individuals exhibited a greater absolute increase in diastolic than in systolic blood but two individuals showed a marked reversal of this trend. The increases in palm conductance ranged from low to high and increases in heart rate were very variable. These results showed that individuals do not show concordant changes in all physiological measures of stress. The study showed that people show organised patterns of somatic response to stress that can be reliably measured and differentiated. The patterning of somatic reaction is as important as average reactivity. The extent to which two individuals differ in autonomic response may depend on which type of physiological variable is used. Lacey's findings became the basis for the theory of individual response-stereotypy.

Example from Psychology of Education

Pendlington (2004) is a case study of a mathematics intervention undertaken with six low-achieving Year 6 children in which the author addressed the problem of self-esteem. When the children (who were all working at least one level below expected level) found a mathematics task too difficult their behavioural responses included crying, becoming silent, refusing to participate and kicking out. The children all used negative labelling to describe themselves and their mathematical ability in comparison to their peers. The researcher worked with the children in a group for 60 hours over a period of 11 weeks. Pendlington described how she changed her teaching approach in response to the disengagement of the pupils when they made an error. Before engaging with the next task she warned them that the task was difficult and that they should expect problems. On this occasion the children worked without behavioural interruptions. When the children were prepared for difficulties they remained engaged but when they were not prepared they became disengaged and behavioural problems ensued. The researcher went on to prioritise affective (mood-changing) strategies. By the end of the project Pendlington found that the children were able to struggle with difficult tasks without affective preparation. The children came to accept that struggling, getting stuck and making errors were a normal part of learning mathematics and did not disengage. When the children returned to class they continued to show engagement and their reading also improved. Five out of the six children achieved the expected level in their SATs at the end of the year.

6.7 Using your knowledge in Unit G544: Answering research methods and issues questions

6.7.1 Laboratory and field experiments (ecological validity)

In this section you will be given guidance on how to answer the research methods and issues question of section B. We will take the experimental method and ecological validity as our example.

Part (a) specimen exam question

To answer part (a) of section B Research Methods and Issues you may need to refer back to Chapter 2, which discusses the strengths and weaknesses of different research methods, and Chapter 3, which explores issues such as ecological validity.

Q (a) Using your knowledge of psychology briefly outline what is meant by ecological validity. (4 marks)

To answer part (a) you should define ecological validity and explain its relationship to overall validity, e.g. it means the extent to which a study is natural, i.e. in its setting, the tasks it reflects, and situations/behaviours that are as close as possible to real life as this increases the validity of the study (meaning that the investigation is measuring what it aims to measure).

Part (b) specimen exam question

Q (b) Describe examples of high ecological validity from any <u>two</u> pieces of psychological research. (8 marks)

To answer part (b) you need to describe two pieces of research that you judge to be high in ecological validity from AS examples or A2 examples from the options you have studied such as those outlined above. You need to be explicit in your description about why the studies chosen are high in ecological validity but you do not need to evaluate.

Hint – observations and field experiments are usually higher in ecological validity than laboratory experiments.

Suggested studies from AS: Piliavin *et al.*; Griffiths.

Suggested studies from A2: a very large range to choose from but you will probably refer to field experiments or observations, e.g. Farrington *et al.* (Forensic); Johansson and Aronsson; Lewinsohn *et al.* (Health and Clinical); Brunelle, Janelle and Tennant (Sport and Exercise); Burroughs-Lange; Ilatov *et al.* (Education).

Here is an example of how you might begin this answer:

A (b) Piliavin *et al.*'s underground Samaritan study is a piece of research that is high in ecological validity. In this study four teams of students conducted a field experiment on the New York subway. One student acted as a 'victim' and staged a collapse between underground stations. Two other students observed bystander reactions and timed how long it took anyone to help the 'victim'. Another student waited in the carriage with instructions to intervene if no one else went to help. The researchers found that in more than 90 per cent of cases another passenger gave help spontaneously. This study is high in ecological validity because it is a well-staged incident in a natural setting. The participants (the passengers) were not informed that they were being observed, which is not very ethical but which raised the level of ecological validity as they really thought that the 'victim' was ill (or drunk). Although the victim was an actor their behaviour must have appeared quite realistic as so many passengers went to help. This confirms the ecological validity of the study.

See whether you can continue with another example, preferably from one of your A2 options. There is no example given here as there are so many studies you could choose from. You should aim to describe the study succinctly and you must remember to highlight the reasons why you regard your chosen study as high in ecological validity.

Here is a specimen part (c) question:

Q (c) Discuss the strengths and limitations of conducting psychological research where ecological validity is low. Use examples of psychological research to support your answer. (12 marks)

To gain full marks on a part (c) question you need to provide at least two strengths and two weaknesses of research that is <u>low</u> in ecological validity. Make sure you read the question carefully. It might be an easy mistake to make to think that this question (like the previous one) was asking you about studies that are <u>high</u> in ecological validity.

Hint – studies that are low in ecological validity are usually laboratory experiments.

Strengths: these may include control of variables, standardisation of procedure, determination of cause and effect, replicability.

Weaknesses: you need to be more specific here than simply restating that the studies are low in ecological validity. You should think about whether the measurement is valid, whether the results are not generalisable, the fact that the measure may be reductionist, etc.

Suggested studies from AS: Loftus and Palmer; Baron-Cohen *et al.*; Bandura *et al.*

Suggested studies from A2: Loftus, Loftus and Messo (Forensic); Berkowitz and Geen (Sport and Exercise); Ausubel (Education).

NB: the laboratory experiment from Health and Clinical (Ruiter *et al.*) has not been selected because it appears for a laboratory experiment to be fairly high in ecological validity.

Here is an example of how you might answer this question:

A (c) Psychological research that is low in ecological validity is generally research conducted using the experimental method, particularly laboratory experiments. One strength of such research is that it is generally subject to a high level of control, which means that potential confounding variables are removed. Lab experiments normally have high control of both participant variables and task variables. Examples of studies that control participant variables well are Baron-Cohen (age- and IQ-matched experimental and control groups) and Bandura (children matched on pre-experiment levels of aggression). Studies that show high control of task variables are Loftus and Palmer and Loftus, Loftus and Messo. In Loftus and Palmer all participants watched the same video clips and answered the same questionnaire with the exception of the critical question. In Loftus, Loftus and Messo all participants watched the same set of slides apart from the one that was manipulated (the IV), that is the slide of the customer who either paid by cheque, or pulled a gun, and all answered the same questionnaire and picked a suspect from the same set of 12 line-up pictures. Another strength of laboratory experiments is that they often provide quantitative data that can be easily analysed and subject to statistical analysis. This enabled Loftus and Palmer to show that the manipulation of the critical verb had a demonstrable effect on participants' recall of speed the cars were travelling at. In Baron-Cohen's study the quantitative data (scores on the Reading the Mind in the Eyes Task) enabled the researchers to show a meaningful difference between mean scores of people with autism and mean scores of normal people and people with Tourette's syndrome.

A weakness of research that is low in ecological validity is that the researcher has only shown a demonstrable effect in the setting of the laboratory and with standardised tasks that are often not very natural. This lack of ecological validity may affect whether the study is useful at all. Although the results of Loftus, Loftus and Messo appear to be reliable, we can question their validity. When seeing still slides of an incident, participants showed that they remembered from one slide the gun rather than the person holding it. However, in a real-life situation there would probably be more time and the witness might first have their attention taken by the gun but they might also have time to take in information about the person carrying the gun as well. Another weakness of research that is low in ecological validity is that experiments often collect quantitative data only. For example it would be interesting in Baron-Cohen's study to have qualitative data on the participants' thoughts when they chose the adjective they thought best fitted the emotion shown in the face as it may not be that they are incorrect for the reasons hypothesised by the experimenters. Also, however well experimenters try to control variables there may still be factors that have not been controlled for and researchers sometimes make big claims from experiments that lack ecological validity simply because they have found a statistical difference between groups. This emphasis on quantitative data can therefore lead to a reductionist view of an issue.

In this specimen answer AS studies and a Forensic example were selected. Have a go at writing your own answer with examples from AS and the A2 options you are studying.

Here is a specimen part (d) question:

Q (d) Compare the ecological validity of laboratory experiments with the ecological validity of field experiments. Use examples of psychological research to support your answer. (8 marks)

To gain full marks on a part (d) question you will need to compare at least two field experiments and two laboratory experiments. You should describe the main points of your chosen studies succinctly but you must focus your argument on the question of ecological validity. The question asks you to compare so you do not need to pick examples that are complete contrasts.

Here is an example of how you might answer (d):

A (d) Laboratory experiments tend to be low in ecological validity. This is because they are usually run in closed settings, carefully select participants and run prescribed tasks that provide limited quantitative data. Field experiments on the other hand are usually higher in ecological validity because they are often conducted in natural settings with no or limited control over participants and little control over how participants react – they control experimenter tasks rather than participant tasks. For example, in Loftus and Palmer all the participants see exactly the same video clips and answer the same questionnaire. However, as an attempt to replicate whether people will remember details of the speed cars were going at before they crashed this would be far removed from what people would experience in real life (e.g. adrenaline rush, trauma) and therefore we cannot generalise the results to what happens to people's memories in a real-life incident. In Piliavin et al. a field experiment was run in a carriage on the New York subway. The main control was the procedure followed by the experimenters, i.e. the 'victim' was programmed to collapse after 70 seconds, the model was programmed to respond after another 70 seconds and the observers took details of what they observed. However, although there was no control over the participants in terms of who got into the carriage, there was control in so far as the passengers could not get off until the next subway station (seven minutes later). This study was higher in ecological validity because the situation was natural but it was again not that generalisable because it is not often in life that you cannot get away from a situation – the main similarities being stuck in a lift or on an aeroplane. This will have lowered the ecological validity of this study even though it was a field experiment and may help explain why 'diffusion of responsibility' was not found. Two experiments that analysed the effect of anger are good examples to illustrate differences in ecological validity between a laboratory and a field experiment. In Berkowitz and Geen the experimenters controlled the procedure. They aroused the participants by giving them mild electric shocks and manipulated the IV such as name of the stooge, which film clip was watched (fight or race), etc. They found that the name of the stooge affected the anger response of the participants. This study was low in ecological validity as nothing in the process was natural so the result is not really valid. In contrast the field experiment run by Brunelle, Janelle and Tennant on anger in soccer players was high in ecological validity. The soccer players were allocated to one of three conditions (anger awareness, role play and control) and then they were observed playing in a number of competitive games for anger expression as well as responding to a self-report measure on anger. Because this was a study of soccer players in real games this study is much higher in ecological validity and enables us to understand anger and anger management better than Berkowitz and Geen's study.

In this specimen answer reference has been made to AS studies and two studies from Sport and Exercise Psychology. Have a go at writing your own answer based on AS studies and research from the A2 applied options you are studying.

Here is a specimen part (e) question:

Q (e) Discuss the usefulness of field experiments in psychology. (8 marks)

When psychologists discuss 'usefulness' they include not only whether the study is of practical use (e.g. can it inform police practice?) but also whether the research is valid (theoretical usefulness). There is no point carrying out a study on an important issue with practical implications such as eyewitness testimony if your findings are invalidated by low ecological validity or lack of replicability. This may highlight the fact that just because a study has high ecological validity does not necessarily mean it is useful.

Examples:

Piliavin et al.: apparently high on ecological validity but not that useful because people were enclosed in a space from which they could not escape. We do not know whether so many people would have helped if they could have easily moved away from the critical area completely.

Farrington, Ditchfield and Joliffe (Forensic): this was a field experiment high in ecological validity because it dealt with actual young offenders and two treatment regimes. Although there is no question over the ecological validity of this study the conclusions drawn were invalidated by the fact that the experimenters were not able to match the experimental groups with controls successfully and instead had to compare predicted/actual reoffending rates of experimental and control groups separately instead of being able to make cross–group comparisons of actual reoffending rates. The way in which predictions were calculated was not reliable and so this greatly reduces the usefulness of this research.

Burroughs-Lange: this field experiment tested the Reading Recovery scheme. This was high in ecological validity because it was an intervention conducted with actual low-reading-ability children in various primary schools. However, it may not be that useful in pinpointing the specific advantages of the Reading Recovery scheme as there was no control on who delivered the different interventions, time spent on the interventions, numbers in intervention groups, etc. In fact this was a field experiment without any controls at all so the results would not necessarily be replicated on another occasion. This means the study is not that reliable or useful.

Examples selected here are from AS, Forensic and Education.

Select some examples of field experiments from the applied options you are studying and have a go at evaluating them.

6.7.2 Observations and experiments (ethics)

You should be able to apply the strategy explained above to answer questions on any combination of research method and issue. In the remaining sections you will be offered guidance rather than specimen answers.

Q (a) Using your knowledge of psychology briefly outline one ethical issue in relation to observational research. (4 marks)

Refer back to Chapter 2, p.28–35 and Chapter 3, p.48–51 to help you answer this question. Likely answers will refer to ethical issues that are difficult to manage in observational research such as informed consent, debrief, deception, etc.

Q (b) Describe ethical issues raised by any two examples of observational research. (8 marks)

In answering this question you may refer to any Core Studies that use the observational method or to any A2 studies that incorporate observations. You should summarise the studies succinctly but concentrate on the ethical issues your examples raise.

Hint: observational research can be pure observations or it can be a method used as part of an experiment. Ethical issues raised by any type of observational research can be discussed here.

Suggested studies from AS: Piliavin *et al.*; Bandura, Ross and Ross.

Suggested studies from A2: Haney, Banks and Zimbardo (Forensic); Lewinsohn *et al.* (Health and Clinical); Brunelle, Janelle and Tennant (Sport and Exercise); Ilatov *et al.* (Education).

Q (c) Discuss the strengths and limitations of conducting psychological research which raises ethical issues. Use examples of psychological research to support your answer. (12 marks)

To gain full marks on a part (c) question you need to provide at least two strengths and two weaknesses of research that raises ethical issues.

Strengths: these may include high ecological validity, naturalistic setting, importance of issues raised, e.g. obedience.

Weaknesses: might cause psychological harm to participants, hard to control variables if participants are unaware they are taking part in a study; use of technology, e.g. MRI, PET, could be damaging; fairness of allocation to interventions/control groups; damage to reputation of psychological research.

Suggested studies from AS: Piliavin; Bandura; Milgram; Savage-Rumbaugh.

Suggested A2 studies: Haney, Banks and Zimbardo; Raine, Buchsbaum and LaCasse (Forensic); Becker *et al.*; Watson and Rayner (Health and Clinical); Berkowitz and Geen; Sparling *et al.* (Health and Clinical); Boaler *et al.*; Ilatov *et al.* (Education).

Q (d) Compare the ethical issues involved in experiments with the ethics involved in observational research. Use examples of psychological research to support your answer. (8 marks)

To gain full marks on a part (d) question you will need to compare at least two experiments with two observations. You should describe the main points of your chosen studies succinctly but you must focus your argument on the nature of the ethical issues involved in the different methods. The question asks you to compare so you do not need to pick examples that are complete contrasts.

Suggested experiments: Milgram, and Berkowitz and Geen – issues deception and psychological harm.

Suggested observations: Piliavin and Bandura (Bandura is also an experiment and that can be a point of discussion) – issues lack of informed consent; psychological harm.

Q (e) Discuss whether psychological research has been harmed by the increasing rigour of ethical guidelines. (8 marks)

This is asking you to think about how much we would have lost without studies like Milgram and Bandura and whether contemporary research is less useful because of the guidelines that psychologists have to follow. An interesting comparison could be made here between Zimbardo's Stanford Prison Experiment and Reicher and Haslam's BBC prison study. Is recent research (undertaken under stricter ethical guidelines) any less valuable than older research? Do you think that the ethical guidelines could be even stricter? For example should the same rigorous standard apply to animal research? Is Savage-Rumbaugh's work unethical? What we would lose if psychologists stopped working with primates?

6.7.3 Self-report and experiments (quantitative/qualitative data)

You should be able to apply the strategy explained above (see 6.7.1) to answer questions on any combination of research method and issue.

Q (a) Define what is meant by qualitative and quantitative data. (4 marks)

Refer back to Chapter 3, p.73–4 to help you answer this question. Likely answers will refer to the fact that qualitative data are descriptive data that provide rich insights into behaviours and feelings while quantitative data are numerical data that can be analysed statistically.

Q (b) Describe two pieces of research in which qualitative data were collected. (8 marks)

In answering this question you may refer to any Core Studies that collect qualitative data or any A2 studies that collect qualitative data. You should summarise the studies succinctly, concentrating mainly on the nature of the data gathered.

Hint: you do not have to cite studies that only collect qualitative data – some studies are mixed method, which means that they collect both quantitative and qualitative data and these can be discussed so long as you concentrate on the qualitative data primarily.

Suggested studies from AS: Freud, Thigpen and Cleckley, Dement and Kleitman (mixed); Milgram (mixed).

Suggested studies from A2: Haney, Banks and Zimbardo (Forensic); Watson and Raynor (Health and Clinical); Turman (Sport and Exercise); Morris; Olweus; Pendlington (Education).

Q (c) Discuss the strengths and limitations of conducting psychological research which produces quantitative data. Use examples of psychological research to support your answer. (12 marks)

To gain full marks on a part (c) question you need to provide at least two strengths and two weaknesses of research that produces quantitative data.

Strengths: these may include the practicality of quantitative data collection – it enables data to be collected from large samples; that quantitative data can be analysed so that results can be compared and tests of statistical significance applied.

Weaknesses: reduces human behaviours to numbers, not as rich as qualitative data; forced choice and closed questions limit respondents' opportunity to express views fully.

Suggested studies from AS: Loftus and Palmer, Baron–Cohen, Samuel and Bryant.

There are a great many studies that collect quantitative data of which just a few have been selected as examples.

Suggested A2 studies: Juby and Farrington; Wikström (Forensic); Wineman; Chamberlain and Zika (Health and Clinical); Harackiewicz *et al.*; Gill and Deeter (Sport and Exercise); Klahr and Nigam, Rittschof and Griffin (Education).

Q (d) Compare the self-report method with the experimental method. Use examples of psychological research to support your answer. (8 marks)

To gain full marks on a part (d) question you will need to compare at least two studies that use self-report and at least two experiments. You should describe the main points of your chosen studies succinctly but you must focus your argument on the nature of the ethical issues involved in the different methods. The question asks you to compare so you do not need to pick examples that are complete contrasts. You may comment that the two methods are not mutually exclusive but that a number of experiments use self-report to collect their data.

Suggested self-report studies (AS); Baron–Cohen *et al.*, Dement and Kleitman.

Suggested experiments(AS): Bandura, Ross and Ross; Samuel and Bryant.

Suggested experiments (A2): you have a wide choice (for examples, see p.142–4).

Suggested self-report studies (A2): you have a wide choice that includes most of the suggested A2 studies above that collect quantitative data.

Q (e) Discuss the usefulness of psychological research that collects qualitative data. (8 marks)

This is asking you to think about the practical usefulness (application) and the theoretical usefulness (generalisability, etc.) of research that produces qualitative data. You might refer to purely qualitative studies such as Freud, Turman, Watson and Raynor or mixed-method studies that provide some qualitative data, e.g. Milgram, and Dement and Kleitman. Most of these studies have very small sample sizes, which limits generalisability. It is hard to define reliability and validity in the context of qualitative research. One way is to triangulate data (this means finding different types of data that support each other) but it is quite rare to find such studies. However, qualitative studies can provide rich insights that may be missed in purely quantitative studies. For example, Turman found contradictory evidence on the effects of coaches picking on people. This would have come out as a meaningless average if it had been quantified but the qualitative method of data collection enabled the researcher to understand that attitudes to such behaviour depended on whether the participant had been personally humiliated or not. The usefulness of qualitative data is easily reduced by investigator bias (e.g. Little Hans's father and Freud) as there is no objective measure used.

6.7.4 Correlation and experiment (snapshot/longitudinal)

You should be able to apply the strategy explained above (see 6.7.1) to answer questions on any combination of research method and issue.

Q (a) Describe briefly the difference between a snapshot study and a longitudinal study. (4 marks)

Refer back to Chapter 3, p.71–72 to help you answer this question. Likely answers will refer to the fact that snapshot studies investigate an issue at one point in time while longitudinal research investigates an issue with the same participants on more than one occasion or over a long period of time.

Q (b) Describe examples of <u>two</u> pieces of psychological research that use the correlational method of analysis. (8 marks)

In answering this question you may refer to any Core Studies that use the correlational method or any A2 studies that use the correlational method. You will find you can answer this question more fully if you use A2 studies. You should summarise the studies succinctly, concentrating mainly on their use of correlation.

Hint – you do not have to cite studies that only explore correlations – some test for difference and correlations, and these can be discussed so long as you concentrate on correlations primarily.

Suggested studies from AS: Maguire *et al.*, Dement and Kleitman.

Suggested studies from A2: there are a great number of A2 studies that explore correlations, e.g. Gudjonsson and Sigurdsson (Forensic); Zalewska-Puchala *et al.* (Health and Clinical); Carron, Bray and Eys (Sport and Exercise); Au, Watkins and Hattie (Education).

Q (c) Discuss the strengths and limitations of conducting correlational research. Use examples of psychological research to support your answer. (12 marks)

To gain full marks on a part (c) question you need to provide at least two examples showing the strength and weaknesses of correlational research.

Strengths: here you will probably include the fact that correlational research allows you to analyse relationships between variables that cannot be manipulated such as health data and self-report data; also correlational research is suitable for longitudinal studies.

Weaknesses: you will probably focus on the fact that correlations cannot demonstrate cause and effect as experiments can.

Suggested studies from AS and A2: as part (b) above.

Q (d) Compare the use of correlations and experiments. Use examples of psychological research to support your answer. (8 marks)

To gain full marks on a part (d) question you will need to compare at least two correlational studies and at least two experiments. You should describe the main points of your chosen studies succinctly but you must focus your argument on the nature of the data collection and analysis, i.e. correlation is about relationships between variables whereas experiments test for effects of IVs.

Suggested AS and A2 correlational studies as part (b) above.

Q (e) Discuss the usefulness of longitudinal studies. (8 marks)

When psychologists discuss 'usefulness' they include not only whether the study is of practical use (e.g. can it inform practice?) but also whether the research is valid (theoretical usefulness). Sometimes a snapshot study does not provide enough information – for example, when investigating change over time. Sometimes longitudinal research if prospective can be used to predict effects when experiments would not be feasible. For example, Farrington's longitudinal Cambridge study allowed researchers to identify risk factors in the situations of young boys that might lead them into crime. These hypotheses were put to the test decades later.

6.7.5 Case study and experiment (reliability/validity) (8 marks)

You should be able to apply the strategy explained (see 6.7.1) above to answer questions on any combination of research methods and issues.

Q (a) Using your knowledge of psychology, describe briefly the characteristics of a case study. (4 marks)

Refer back to pp.146–7 to help you answer this question. Likely answers will refer to the fact that a case study usually deals with one participant or a small number and does not apply the experimental method but instead enables the researcher to collect rich, qualitative data.

Q (b) Describe examples of <u>two</u> pieces of psychological research that use the case-study method. (8 marks)

In answering this question you may refer to any Core Studies that use the case study method or any A2 studies that are case studies. You should summarise the studies succinctly, concentrating mainly on what makes them case studies.

Suggested studies from AS: Freud, Thigpen and Cleckley, Dement and Kleitman (mixed); Milgram (mixed).

Suggested studies from A2: Haney, Bank and Zimbardo (Forensic); Watson and Raynor (Health and Clinical); Turman (Sport and Exercise); Morris; Olweus; Pendlington (Education).

Q (c) Discuss the strengths and limitations of case studies. Use examples of psychological research to support your answer. (12 marks)

To gain full marks on a part (c) question you need to provide at least two strengths and two weaknesses of case studies.

Strengths: these may include rich, qualitative data, possibly high ecological validity, possible longitudinal research.

Weaknesses: small sample size, generalisability issues, lack of quantitative data.

Suggested AS and A2 studies as part (b) above.

Q (d) Compare validity issues in case studies and experiments. Use examples of psychological research to support your answer.

To gain full marks on a part (d) question you will need to discuss validity issues and support your argument with at least two examples of case studies and two experiments. You should describe the main points of your chosen studies succinctly but you must focus your argument on the nature of the question of validity. This can include face validity, ecological validity and reliability. The question asks you to compare so you do not need to pick examples that are complete contrasts.

Suggested AS and A2 case studies as part (b) above.

Suggested AS and A2 experiments as above (6.2.1). (8 marks)

Q (e) Discuss the usefulness of psychological research that uses case studies. (8 marks)

When psychologists discuss 'usefulness' they include not only whether the study is of practical use (e.g. can it inform practice?) but also whether the research is valid (theoretical usefulness). There is no point carrying out a study on an important issue with practical implications if your findings are invalidated by lack of replicability or lack of generalisability. Case studies tend to lack these features but you may decide they are useful for other reasons (provide insights into motivations and feelings not accessible through the experimental method).

Bibliography

Akers, R A, Krohn, M D, Lanza-Kaduce, L and Radosevich, M (1979). Social Learning and deviant behaviour: a specific test of a general theory. *American Sociological Review* 44, 636–55

Au, R C P, Watkins, D A and Hattie, J A C (2010). Academic risk factors and deficits of learned hopelessness: a longitudinal study of Hong Kong secondary school students. *Educational Psychology* 30 (2), 125–38

Ausubel, D P (1960). The use of advance organizers in the learning and retention of meaningful verbal material. *Journal of Educational Psychology* 51, 267–72

Bandura, A, Ross, D and Ross, S A (1961). Transmission of aggression through imitation of aggressive models. *Journal of Abnormal and Social Psychology* 63, 371–8

Baron-Cohen, S, Joliffe, T, Mortimer, C and Robertson, M (1997). Another advanced test of theory of mind: evidence from very high functioning adults with autism or Asperger Syndrome. *Journal of Child Psychology and Psychiatry* 38, 813–22

Becker, M H, Radius, S M, Rosenstock, I M, Drachman, R H, Schuberth, K H, and Teets, K C (1978). Compliance with a medical regimen for asthma; a test of the Health Belief Model. *Public Health Reports* 93 (3)

Berkowitz, L and Geen, R G (1966). Film violence and the cue properties of available targets. *Journal of Personality and Social Psychology* 3 (5), 525–30

Bernstein, L, Henderson, B E, Hanisch, R, Sullivan-Halley, J and Ross, R K (1994). Physical exercise and reduced risk of breast cancer in young women. *Journal of the National Cancer Institute* 86 (18), 1403–8

Boaler, J, William D and Brown, M (2000), Students' experiences of ability grouping – disaffection, polarisation and construction of failure, *British Educational Research Journal* 26 (5), 631–48

Brunelle, J P, Janelle, Tennant, L K (1999). Controlling competitive anger among male soccer players. *Journal of Applied Sport Psychology* 11, 283–97

Bruner, J S (1960). *The Process of Education*. Cambridge: Harvard University Press

Budzynski, T H, Stoyva, J M, Adler, C S and D (1973). EMG biofeedback and tension headache: A controlled outcome study. *Psychosomatic Medicine*, 35, 484–96

Burroughs-Lange, S (2008). Comparison of literacy progress of young children in London schools: a Reading Recovery follow up study, published on-line. London, ULIE

Carron, A V, Bray, S R and Eys, M A (2002). Team cohesion and team success in sport. *Journal of Sports Sciences* 20, 119–26

Caspi, A *et al.* (2003). Influence of life stress on depression. Moderation by a polymorphism in the 5-HTT 2 gene. *Science* 301 (5631), 386–9

Chamberlain, K and Zika, S (1990). The minor events approach to stress: support for the use of daily hassles. *British Journal of Psychology* 81, 469–81

Chen, C-A and Howitt, D (2007). Different crime types and moral reasoning development in young offenders compared with non-offender controls. *Psychology, Crime and Law* 13 (4), 405–16

Clark, R D (1998). Minority influence: the role of the rate of majority defection and persuasive arguments. *European Journal of Social Psychology*, 28, 787–96

Coakley, J (1992). Burnout among adolescent athletes: a personal failure or social problem? *Sociology of Sport Journal* 9 (3), 271–85

Dement, W and Kleitman, N (1957). The relation of eye movements during sleep to dream activity: An objective method for the study of dreaming. *Journal of Experimental Psychology* 53, 339–46

Erickson *et al.* (2007), Sport experiences, milestones, and educational activities associated with high-performance coaches' development. *The Sport Psychologist* 21, 302–16

Eysenck, H J, Nias, D K B and Cox, D N (1982). Sport and personality. *Journal of Advances in Behavioural Research and Therapy* 4, 1–56

Farrington, D P, Ditchfield, J, Howard, P and

Joliffe, D (2002). Two intensive regimes for young offenders: a follow-up evaluation. *Home Office, Research, Development and Statistics Directorate, Research Findings 163,* 1–4

Freud, S (1909). Analysis of a phobia in a five-year old boy. *The Standard Edition of the Complete Works of Sigmund Freud.* London: Hogarth, vol 10

Gill, D L and Deeter, T E (1988). Development of the sport orientation questionnaire. *Research Quarterly for Exercise and Sport* 59 (3), 191–202

Griffiths, M D (1994). The role of cognitive bias and skill in fruit machine gambling. *British Journal of Psychology* 85, 351–69

Gudjonsson, G H and Mackeith, J A (1990). A proven case of false confession: psychological aspects of the coerced-compliant type. *Medical Science Law* 30 (4), 329–35

Gudjonsson, G H and Sigurdsson, J F (2007). Motivation for offending and personality. A study among young offenders on probation. *Personality and Individual Differences* 42, 1243–53

Haney, C, Banks, W C and Zimbardo, P G (1973). Study of prisoners and guards in a simulated prison. *Naval Research Reviews* 9, 1–17

Harackiewicz, J M, Barron, K E, Carter, S M, and Lehto, A T (1997), Predictors and consequences of achievement goals in the college classroom: maintaining interest and making the grade. *Journal of Personality and Social Psychology* 73 (6), 1284–95

Heller, K A (2004). Identification of Gifted and Talented Students. *Psychology Science,* 46 (3), 302–23

Ilatov, Z, Shamai, S, Hertz-Lazarovitz, R and Mayer-Young, S (1998). Teacher–student classroom interactions: the influence of gender, academic dominance, and teacher communication style. *Adolescence* 33 (130), 269–77

Johansson, G and Aronsson, G (1984). Stress reactions in computerized administrative work. *Journal of Occupational Behaviour* 5, 159–81

Juby, H and Farrington, D P (2001). Disentangling the link between disrupted families and delinquency. *British Journal of Criminology,* 41 (1), 22–40

Kendler, K S, MacLean, C, Neale, M, Kessler, R, Heath, A and Eaves, L (1991). The genetic epidemiology of Bulimia Nervosa. *American Journal of Psychiatry* 148, 1627–37

Kimura, D (2002). Sex differences in the brain. *Scientific American Special Edition,* 12 (1), 32–7

Klahr, D and Nigam, M (2004). The equivalence of learning paths in early science instruction: effects of direct instruction and discovery learning. *Psychological Science* 15 (10), 661–7

Lacey, J I (1950), Individual differences in somatic response patterning. *Journal of Comparative and Physiological Psychology* 43, 338–50

Lewinsohn, P M, Mischel, W, Chaplin, W and Narton, R (1980). Social competence and depression: the role of illusory self perceptions. *Journal of Abnormal Behaviour* 89 (2), 203–12

Loftus, E F, Loftus, G R and Messo, J (1987). Some facts about weapon focus. *Journal of Law and Human Behaviour* 11 (1), 55–62

Loftus, E F and Palmer, J C (1974). Reconstruction of automobile destruction: an example of the interaction between language and memory. *Journal of Verbal Learning and Verbal Behaviour* 13, 585–9

Maguire, E A, Gadian, N G, Johnsrude, I S, Good, C D, Ashburner, J, Frackowiak, R S and Frith, C D (2000). Navigation-related structural changes in the hippocampi of taxi drivers. *Proceedings of the National Academy of Sciences* 97 (8), 4398–403

Milgram, S (1963). Behavioural study of obedience. *Journal of Abnormal and Social Psychology* 67, 371–8

Morris, E W (2005). Tuck in that shirt! Race, class, gender and discipline in an urban school. *Sociological Perspectives* 48 (1), 25–48

Munroe-Chandler, K, Hall, C and Fishburne, G (2008). Playing with confidence: the relationship between imagery use and self-confidence and self-efficacy in youth soccer players. *Journal of Sports Sciences* 26 (14), 1539–46

Olweus, D (1991), Bully/victim problems in school: Facts and intervention. *European Journal of Psychology of Education* 12 (4), 495–510

Palmer, E J and Connelly, R (2005). Depression, hopelessness and suicide ideation among vulnerable prisoners. *Criminal Behaviour and Mental Health,* 15 (3), 164–70

Palmer, E J and Hollin, C R (2004a). Predicting reconviction using the Psychological Inventory of Criminal Thinking Styles with English prisoners. *Legal and Criminological Psychology* 9 (1), 57–68

Palmer, E J and Hollin, C R (2004b). The use of the Psychological Inventory of Criminal Thinking Styles with English young offenders. *Legal and Criminological Psychology*, 9 (2), 253–63

Pendlington, S (2004). Low self-esteem: its effect on low achievers learning, in: Noyes, A (ed.), *Proceedings of the British Society for Research into Learning Mathematics* 24 (3)

Piaget, J (1952/1936). *The Origins of Intelligence in Children*. New York: International University Press

Piliavin, I M, Rodin, J A and Piliavin, J (1969). Good Samaritanism: An underground phenomenon? *Journal of Personality and Social Psychology* 13, 289–99

Raine, A, Buchsbaum, M and LaCasse, L (1997). Brain abnormalities in murderers indicated by Positron Emission Tomography. *Biological Psychiatry* 42 (6), 495–508

Reicher, S D and Haslam, S A (2006).Rethinking the psychology of tyranny: The BBC prison study. *British Journal of Social Psychology* 45, 1–40

Rittschof, K A and Griffin, B W (2001). Reciprocal peer tutoring: re-examining the value of a co-operative learning technique to college students and instructors. *Educational Psychology* 21 (3), 313–31

Rosenhan, D L (1973). On being sane in insane places. *Science* 179 (70), 250–8

Ruiter, R A C, Kok, G, Verplanken, B and Brug, J (2001). Evoked fear and effects of appeals on attitudes to performing breast self-examination: an information-processing perspective. *Health Education Research. Theory and Practice* 16 (3)

Samuel, J and Bryant, P (1984). Asking only one question in the conservation experiment. *Journal of Child Psychology* 22 (2), 315–18

Savage-Rumbaugh, S, McDonald, K, Sevcik, R A, Hopkins, W D and Rubert, E (1986). Spontaneous symbol acquisition and communicative use by Pygmy chimpanzees (Pan paniscus). *Journal of Experimental Psychology* 115 (3), 211–35

Seligman, M E P (1974). Depression and learned helplessness. In: Friedman, R J and Katz, M M (eds). *The Psychology of Depression: contemporary theory and research*. Washington, DC: Winston Wiley

Sinha, S P, Nayyar, P and Sinha, S P (2002). Social support and self-control as variables in attitude toward life and perceived control among older people in India. *Journal of Social Psychology* 142 (4), 527–40

Skinner, B F (1953). *Science and human behaviour*. New York: Macmillan

Sparling, P B, Giujrida, A, Piomelli, D, Rosskopf, L and Dietrich, A (2003). Exercise activates the endocannabinoid system. *Neuroreport* 14 (17), 2209–11

Sperry, R W (1968). Hemisphere deconnection and unity in conscious awareness. *American Psychologist* 23, 723–33

Thigpen, C and Cleckley, H (1957). A case of multiple personality disorder. *Journal of Abnormal and Social Psychology* 49, 135–51

Turman, P D (2003), Coaches and cohesion: the impact of coaching techniques on team cohesion in the small group sport setting. *Journal of Sport Behavior* 26 (1), 86–104

Vygotsky, L (1933; English translation, 1966). Play and its role in the mental development of the child. *Voprosy psikhologii*, 6 (trans. C Mulholland). Psychology and Marxism Internet Archive (marxists.org) 2002.

Watson, J B and Rayner, R (1920), Conditioned emotional reactions. *Journal of Experimental Psychology*, 3, 1–14

Whittington, C J, Kendall, T, Fonagy, P, Cottrell, D, Cotgrove, A and Boddington, E (2004). Selective serotonin reuptake inhibitors in childhood depression: systematic review of published versus unpublished data. *The Lancet*, 363, 1341–5

Wikström, P-E H (2003). Individual Risk, Life-Style Risk, and Adolescent Offending: Findings from the Peterborough Youth Study. *Report of the work of the Institute of Criminology*, 1–5

Wineman, N M (1980). Obesity: Locus of control, body image, weight loss and age-at-onset. *Nursing Research* , 29 (4), 231–7

Zalewksa-Puchala, J, Majda, M, Galuszka, A and Kolonko, J (2007). Health behaviour of students versus a sense of self-efficacy. *Advances in Medical Sciences* 32, 73–7

Index

aggression, studies of 14, 25, 126
allocation, of participants 24
    see also experimental design; sampling
alternate (experimental) hypothesis 18, 25, 41, 56, 107–8
anonymity 50, 83
    see also ethics
Au, R.C.P. 145
Ausubel, D.P. 128
averages *see* measures of central tendency
avoidance of harm 48–9
    see also ethics

Bandura, A. 12, 14, 20, 25, 30–2, 41
bar charts 79
Baron-Cohen, S. 4, 22, 41, 57, 71, 76
behaviourism 12–14, 121, 123, 125, 128, 138–9
Berkowitz, L. 125
Bernstein, L. 124
biological approach *see* physiological approach
boredom effects 27
brain-scanning studies 6, 41, 119, 126–7
Brunelle, J.P. 143
Budzynski, T.H. 147
Burroughs-Lange, S. 144, 153

Carron, A.V. 124
case study method 3, 146–8
catharsis 126
cause and effect 3, 40–1, 58
central tendency, measures of 19, 75–8
children
    consent of 49
    developmental studies 12, 147–8
    see also educational psychology
Chi-square test 109
Clark, R.D. 119–20
classical conditioning 123, 125
clinical psychology *see* health and clinical psychology
closed questions 38, 39
Coakley, J. 125
cognitive psychology 2–5, 119, 121, 123–4, 126, 130–4
computer software, for data analysis 73

concordance 33
    see also statistical tests
confederate (stooge) 30
confidentiality 50
    see also ethics
confounding variables 26–7, 44, 60
    see also reliability
consent 49, 80
    see also ethics
content analysis 73
control, of variables 18, 20–1, 44
controlled observations 30, 45
correlational analysis 13, 40–3, 47, 145
correlational investigation, procedure for 104
counterbalancing 27
    see also experimental design
covert observations 31, 33, 45
crime *see* forensic psychology
cross-sectional (snapshot) studies 71–2
culture 129, 133

data
    distribution of 108
    levels of measurement 106–7
    qualitative 73–4
    quantitative 73–5
data analysis 73–9
    computer software 73
    graphical representations 40, 42, 47, 79
    inferential/statistical tests 107–9
    measures of central tendency 19, 75–8
    measures of dispersion 79
    see also correlational analysis
debates, in psychology 118, 128–30
debrief 50, 83
deception 49, 81
    see also ethics
demand characteristics 33
Dement, W. 6, 7, 22
dependent variable (DV) 18, 19–20, 58–9
depression, studies of 120, 122–3
descriptive data *see* qualitative data
descriptive statistics 75–9
    see also data analysis
determinism 129

developmental psychology 11–13, 120, 122–3, 125, 128, 137–8
distribution, of data 108

ecological validity 5, 23, 33, 54–6, 85–6, 150–3
educational psychology 126–8, 144, 145, 147–8
Erikson, E. 128
ethics 48–50, 102, 153–4
    avoidance of harm 48–9
    confidentiality/anonymity 50, 83
    debrief 50, 83
    deception 49, 81
    informed consent 49, 80
    right to withdraw 49, 82
ethnocentrism 129, 133
event sampling 32, 35, 45
    see also time sampling
exercise psychology see sport and exercise
    psychology
experimental design 24–7
experimental hypothesis 18, 25, 41, 56, 107–8
experiments 17–27
    field 9, 21, 142–4, 151–2
    laboratory 18, 21, 143, 150–1
    procedures for 66, 68–9, 90–1
    quasi 6–7, 21–2
    see also experimental design
extraneous variables 26–7, 44, 60
Eysenck, H.J. 125

face validity 51–2, 101
Farrington, D.P. 142, 152
field experiments 9, 21, 142–4, 151–2
forensic psychology 119–21, 142, 145, 146
free will 129
Freud, S. 12, 15, 126

gender studies 126–7
graphical representation, of data 40, 42, 47, 79
Griffiths, M.D. 10, 31, 32
group cohesion, study of 124
Gudjonsson, G.H. 145, 146

harm, avoidance of 48–9
health and clinical psychology 121–3, 143, 147
Heller, K.A. 127
holism 129

hypotheses
    accepting/rejecting 107–8
    alternate (experimental) 18, 25, 41, 56, 107–8
    in correlational analysis 41–2
    null 18, 25, 42, 56, 107–8
    one-tailed 56–7, 99
    operationalising 56–7, 98–9
    p-value 107
    research questions 96–8
    two-tailed 56–7, 99
    Type 1 error 107–8
    Type 2 error 108

Ilatov, Z. 127
independent-measures design 24, 26–7
independent variable (IV) 18–19, 58–9
individual differences approach 10–11, 120, 122, 124–5, 127, 136–7
individual versus situational explanations 129
inferential tests 107–9
    see also data analysis
informed consent 49, 80
    see also ethics
inter-observer reliability 33
interval-level data 106
interviews 37
    see also self-report method

Johansson, G. 143

Kendler, K.S. 121–2
Kimura, D. 126–7
Klahr, D. 126

laboratory experiments 18, 21, 143, 150–1
Lacey, J.I. 147
Lewinsohn, P.M. 122
literacy, studies of 144, 153
    see also educational psychology
Loftus, E.F. 3, 19–21, 24, 48–9, 119
longitudinal studies 71–2, 157

Maguire, E.A. 6, 41, 42
Mann–Whitney U test 109
matched-participants design 25–6
mean 19–20, 76
measurement, levels of 106–7

measures of central tendency 19, 75–8
measures of dispersion 79
median 19, 76
Milgram, S. 9, 13–14
minority influence, in juries 119–20
mode 19, 77
Munroe-Chandler, K. 123–4

natural observations 30, 45
nature-nurture debate 129
nominal data 106
non-parametric tests 108–9
   see also data analysis
normal distribution 108
null hypothesis 18, 25, 42, 56, 107–8

objectivity 5
   see also subjectivity
observations 9, 28–34
   controlled 30, 45
   covert/overt 31, 33, 45
   event sampling 32, 35, 45
   inter-observer reliability 33
   natural 30, 45
   participant 30, 45
   procedures for 66–8, 89–90, 105
   recording 32
   structured/unstructured 31–2, 45
   time sampling 32, 35, 45
offender studies see forensic psychology
one-tailed hypotheses 56–7, 99
open questions 38
operationalising
   hypotheses 56–7, 98–9
   variables 58
opportunity sampling 61, 64–5
order effects 27
ordinal data 106
overt observations 31, 33, 45

Palmer, E.J. 120
participant observations 30, 45
participant variables 26–7, 44
participants
   allocation of 24
   anonymity 50, 83
   boredom effects 27
   consent 49, 80

debriefing 50, 83
demand characteristics 33
order effects 27
practice effects 27
right to withdraw 49, 82
stress 23, 48–9
   see also ethics; sampling
Pendlington, S. 147–8
physical correlates 5
physiological approach 5–8, 119, 121–2, 124,
   126–7, 134–5
Piaget, J. 53
Piliavin, I.M. 9, 20–1, 30
positive reinforcement 128
   see also classical conditioning
practice effects 27
probability 107
procedure
   correlational investigation 104
   experiments 66, 68–9, 90–1, 99–102
   longitudinal versus snapshot 71–2
   observations 66–8, 89–90, 105
   self-report method 66, 69–70, 91–2, 103
   steps for practical investigation 65–6
psychodynamic perspective 15–16, 125–6, 139–40
psychology as science 130
p-value 107

qualitative data 73–4
quantitative data 73–5
quasi-experiments 6–7, 21–2
questionnaires 38–9, 123–4, 145
   see also self-report method

Raine, A. 119
random allocation, of participants 24
random sampling 61–2, 64, 89, 101
range (the) 79
ratio data 107
Reading Recovery study 144, 153
reductionism 129
Reicher, S.D. 9, 22
relationships, establishing see correlational analysis
reliability 20, 27, 51–4, 60, 101
   inter-observer 33
   see also confounding variables; validity
repeated-measures design 25, 26–7
replication 17

see also reliability; validity
research question, selection and construction 96–8
  see also hypotheses
right to withdraw 49, 82
  see also ethics
Rosenhan, D.L. 11
Ruiter, R.A.C. 143

sampling 60–5, 87–8, 100–1
  event 32, 35
  opportunity 61, 64–5
  random 61–2, 64, 89, 101
  self-selecting 62, 64, 100
  time 32, 35
Samuel, J. 12, 18, 20–1, 25, 53
Savage-Rumbaugh, S. 4, 32
scattergraphs 40, 42, 47
scientific method 17, 28, 132
  see also experiments
self-efficacy, studies of 121, 122
self-report method 10, 36–9, 145
  and children 12
  interviews 37
  procedures for 66, 69–70, 91–2, 103
  questionnaires 38–9
self-selecting sampling 62, 64, 100
sign tests 109
  see also data analysis
significance, levels of 107
Sinha, S.P. 122
snapshot (cross-sectional) studies 71–2
social psychology 8–10, 119, 122, 124, 127, 135–6
Spearman's rank correlation coefficient 109
Sperry, R.W. 6, 7
sport and exercise psychology 123–6, 143–4, 147
Sport Imagery Questionnaire for Children 123–4
SSRIs (selective serotonin reuptake inhibitors),
  study of 123
statistical significance 107
statistical tests 107–9
  see also data analysis
stooge (confederate) 30
stress
  in participants 23, 48–9
  studies of 122, 143, 147
structured observations 32, 45
subjectivity 5, 38

task variables 26–7, 44
theories, proving/disproving 17
  see also hypotheses
Thigpen, C. 15, 37
time sampling 32, 35, 45
  see also event sampling
twin studies 122
two-tailed hypotheses 56–7, 99
Type 1 error 107–8
Type 2 error 108

unstructured observations 31, 45
'usefulness' of psychological research 130, 157–8

validity 20, 51–4, 101
  ecological 5, 23, 33, 54–6, 85–6, 150–3
  face 51–2, 101
  see also reliability
variables 3
  confounding 26–7, 44, 60
  control of 18, 20–1, 44
  correlated 3
  dependent (DV) 18, 19–20, 58–9
  independent (IV) 18–19, 58–9
  operationalising 58–9
  participant 26–7, 44
  task 26–7, 44
volunteer sampling *see* self-selecting sampling

Watson, J.B. 123
Whittington, C.J. 123
Wilcoxon signed-ranks test 109
withdrawal, of participants 49, 82

Zalewska-Puchala, J. 121